Published by Stereo Output Limited, company number 11174059

ISBN number 978-1-9996003-0-3

Copyright © Ashley Hewitt 2018

Ashley Hewitt has asserted his right under the Copyright, Designs
and Patents Act 1988 to be identified as the author of this work.

All rights reserved. No part of this publication may be reproduced,
stored in a retrieval system, or transmitted in any form or by any
means, electronic, mechanical, photocopying, recording or
otherwise, without the prior permission of the copyright holder
except in the case of brief quotations embodied in critical views and
certain other non-commercial uses permitted by copyright law.

Thank you to Rej at Single Cell Software for the permission to
profile Caustic so extensively.

Please go to www.stereooutput.com to contact us or follow us on
various social media channels.

Dedicated to Michael Hewitt, Juliet Dover and Natalie Krisman –
thank you for your ongoing inspiration and support.

Preface

This book was conceived as a consequence of a long time spent struggling with synthesizers, be it hardware or software. Most producers want to stop using presets and fashion their own palette of sounds, but find that even if they create a beautiful sound by accident, the subsequent recreation of that sound is out of reach.

I believe that this is due to an unstructured knowledge of how synthesizers work. This book was written to give you the ability to adapt to and work with any synthesizer that you happen across, freeing you to make the beautiful music that you've always wanted to create.

In the same way that there are different cars, there are different synthesizers, all of which work slightly differently. They all, however, possess the same underlying structure. If you have the correct mental toolkit, you will quickly be able to adapt to any new synthesizer you come across. This book will provide you with that mental toolkit.

A common criticism of synthesizer teaching resources is that they only provide information as to how to work one specific model of synth, and not whichever synthesizer the user possesses.

Unfortunately, it's not possible to account for all models of synthesizer in one book. It's also very easy, when struggling to understand synthesis, to flit from synthesizer to synthesizer, only understanding its most basic functions, never getting to know a synthesizer in depth.

Therefore, this book's lessons are entirely based on one synthesizer – Caustic's SubSynth. The reason I've chosen SubSynth is that it's a simple, basic subtractive synthesizer (i.e. you pick a waveform or two, and then shape it afterwards). It does everything reasonably well, with no bells and whistles, and is therefore a perfect synthesizer to learn with.

It is available on a music-making platform called Caustic, which is cheap and available for virtually any computing platform you own. As of writing, it's available on Android and iOS through their respective App stores, and available on, PC and Mac at http://www.singlecellsoftware.com/caustic. I strongly suggest you acquire it before you begin the exercises in this book.

If you truly can't get hold of Caustic, other simple computer-based synthesizers that would enable to you to follow the instructions in this book include:

· Reason's Subtractor synth
· Logic Pro X's Retro Synth (use the analog mode)
· Ableton's Analog
· Blaukraut Engineering's free Charlatan synth (Windows only)
· TAL's free Elek7ro

However, if you are not using Caustic, transferring the knowledge from the synthesizer in this book to whatever synthesizer you're using may be difficult. Embrace that difficulty as part of the fun. This book is all about getting hands-on with whatever gear you're using and working things out for yourself, applying the knowledge gleaned from this book. At the same time, don't expect it to be *too* difficult! Synthesizers have not changed drastically in the decades since they've been invented, and this is testament to their intuitive design.

Feeling uncomfortable transferring one's knowledge from one synthesizer to another, in my eyes, is merely a product of lacking structured knowledge. All synthesizers use a very similar design, and have done so for decades – and transferring your knowledge from one synthesizer to another is easy if you understand the functions of all the different parts of the synthesizer and how they fit together. This book will furnish you with this knowledge.

I make no assumptions as to your level of knowledge as a reader, so if you have a background in music technology, you may already know some (or even lots) of the theory referred to in the book. If that is the case, then there's no harm in confirming what you already know! I'd much rather an experienced music technologist be forced to skim some of the simpler parts of this book than have someone with little experience be forced to fill in knowledge gaps outside of this book.

Before we start, it's worth explaining the nomenclature of this book. There are two main controls that we'll be using in Caustic's SubSynth - and these types of control happen to be prevalent in many electronic devices.

The sound experiments in this book will explore the full spectrum of sounds that subtractive synthesizers have to offer, so a better audio setup will give you better results. Even a decent pair of headphones plugged into your device will work – just don't rely on phone speakers!

Pots are circular controls such as this one:

I refer to the position of the indicator on the pot by the time it shows if it was on a clock. For example, the pot above would be at midday. The pot below would be at 3 o'clock:

In addition to pots, there are sliders. This is a slider:

I tend to refer to sliders as to their location - I'd refer to the above slider as being halfway up.

In addition to learning the nomenclature of all the different parts of a synthesizer, you will also be set exercises at the end of most chapters. These will either be in the form of practice or a Q&A. The answers to the Q&A are in Appendix A. If you're using an electronic version of the book, there will be a link to Appendix A at the end of each chapter and a link back to the chapter within the answers.

Hopefully by now, you've installed Caustic on whatever device you intend to be using, and you're sat with baited breath, ready to program some beauty into your synthesizer. Let's dive in – but not before we have learned some theory.

Chapter 1 – What is sound?

What is sound?

It's an almost infuriatingly simple question, isn't it?

However, a synthesizer at its very basic level is a sound generator. In order to harness its power to the best of its ability, it's important to understand what sound is, and how it works.

Sound is a pressure wave that ripples out from a source (e.g. a drum being struck). This pressure wave is picked up by a tiny membrane within your ear called an eardrum, through which the signal is passed, via some intricate biological mechanisms, to your brain – which translates the signal into the sound perceived.

The three most important properties of sound waves, as they pertain to synthesis, are frequency, amplitude and waveform. The following graphic represents all three:

These three properties are explained below:

1) Amplitude. This is how big the sound wave is. Bigger sound waves sound louder, smaller sound waves sound quieter.

2) Frequency. This is how often a wave reaches its trough (i.e. hits the bottom of its cycle). It is measured in Hertz, which is how many of these troughs occur per second. Hertz, when written, is generally shortened to Hz. Even if you haven't heard of Hertz in the context of music, you will have heard of it in other contexts. For example, tuning an analogue radio to 252kHz means you're tuning it to a radio wave frequency of 252,000 cycles per second (which, in itself, is quite mind blowing).

3) Waveform. Waveform is the actual shape of the sound wave. This affects what the sound is perceived as. For example, this is a waveform of a synthesized kick drum:

Whereas this is the waveform of someone saying 'hello':

Do you notice the differences between the two? It's those differences that allow your brain to discern the sound of the kick drum from the sound of the voice saying 'hello'.

As stated, sound waves are measured in cycles per second, or Hertz. A sound at less than 20 cycles per second is imperceptible to the human ear, as your brain will discern each vibration individually. At the same time, a sound at more than 20,000 Hertz is imperceptible to the human ear (but perceptible to some other species of mammal). To illustrate the lower end of the range of human hearing, simply get into a car and start it. You'll notice that as the engine ticks over, you can hear each tick individually. However, once you rev the engine to a certain point, you're no longer able to hear the individual ticks – you will instead hear what sounds like a low tone that increases in frequency with the rev count. This is because the speed at which the engine is turning has increased beyond 20 cycles per second. i.e. the threshold of your hearing.

The reason the basic properties of sound relate so well to synthesis is that a synthesizer allows you to select a basic waveform, then precisely alter the frequency, amplitude and waveform of that sound – to a far greater extent than if you were playing an acoustic guitar, for example. As you work through this book, I suggest you analyse the functions of the synthesizer and think about how they relate to the properties of sound perception.

The synthesizer delivers sound in a very simple manner, too. Imagine a plane flying past your window. The plane generates sound waves that are sensed by your ears:

When you're using a synthesizer, the synthesizer generates audio waves, which are converted to sound pressure waves using your speakers. It is these waves that are subsequently sensed by your ears.

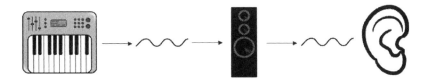

That a synthesizer could directly create audio waves was deemed very important as it was invented in its many iterations over the course of the early to middle 20th century. The implications were that rather than undertake the difficult task of convincing an orchestra to play their piece at a concert, a synthesizer could play their compositions back to them at a far lesser cost. The idea at the time was that if a synthesizer could be programmed to precisely emulate, for example, the waveform of a violin, asking a violin player to play their piece would not be necessary.

As we know from listening to synthesizer music, it did not work out like this - even now in the 21st century, no-one has quite managed the precise emulation of an entire orchestra. However, what came from synthesis was far more interesting – an entirely novel set of instruments, each with their own sound and timbre.

The spread of Digital Audio Workstation software on cheap computing hardware in the 90s has helped the innovators of the 20th century realise their utopian ideals, but in reference to contemporary music. It is now possible for anyone, with a small amount of money, to compose and listen to their own music in the comfort of their own home – as long as they don't want to hear it on a symphony orchestra!

I hope the beauty of synthesis has been made clear in this chapter – rather than use an instrument that creates a waveform through its physical shape (like a guitar, or drum), you're using an instrument that allows you to design and manipulate pure, basic sound waves. You're sitting in front of a method of music-making that, 100 years ago, was beyond the wildest dreams of musicians, and at very little cost.

Thank you for joining me for the journey ahead – now let's get started!

Chapter 1 Exercises – Q&A

1) What is sound?
2) What are the three most important properties of sound waves, as they pertain to synthesis?

3) In what unit is frequency measured?

4) What specifically does Hertz measure?

5) In Hertz, roughly what is the human range of hearing?

If you need any help, the answers are in <u>Appendix A</u>.

Chapter 2 – Active listening

In my time as a music producer, there is one skill that surpasses all others in terms of its use to accelerate your development as a musician. If you're an experienced music producer, you may do it already – however, if you're just getting started, then this, in my opinion, is the most important skill you could acquire as a music producer. It's called **active listening**.

We all listen to music, often while doing work, sitting on the train or cooking food. However, this music often simply provides a background noise to the activity we're doing. I would call this passive listening.

Active listening, on the other hand, is a different beast. To actively listen is to listen to music and hear nothing but the music, concentrating on nothing but the music you're listening to, dissecting and reverse-engineering every layer of the music you're hearing in order to unlock its secrets.

It's a skill that, once practiced, will stay with you forever as a producer. It also goes hand-in-hand with your journey of development as a music producer, in that as you gain experience in music production techniques, you will better spot the techniques that other producers have used.

It is also a skill that becomes easier with practice – it might feel difficult the first time you do it, but with enough attempts you will find yourself applying elements of active listening every time you hear music.

Active listening is an essential skill for this book. I'm sure you've heard basslines in music that you'd define as "deep", "heavy" or "dirty" – this book aims to start you on your journey to knowing what those attributes translate to in the reality of synthesizer programming.

This chapter will conclude with an exercise – an active listening exercise! Even if you're used to actively listening, you should undertake this exercise, as it's always good to refresh your skills in this area.

Exercises – Practice

1) Find a song you want to actively listen to. This could be your favourite song, or one you admire for its sound.
2) Sit comfortably, wearing good-quality headphones or using studio monitors.
3) Eliminate all distractions around you. Turn off your computer monitor, turn your phone over – turn your lights off and close your eyes if possible.
4) Find the best-quality sound source you can – be it vinyl, CD or FLAC/WAV file.

5) Play the song. Instead of enjoying it for what it is, listen to it as a set of different layers. Break them down - listen to each instrument at a time. Are you aware of all the instrument layers in the track? You may discover layers you were previously unaware were of in the track!

6) Play the song again. Does the song change its narrative tone at any point? If so, how is this accomplished?

7) What texture does the song have? Does the texture change at any point in the track?

I hope you enjoyed your active listening session, whether it was your first or one of many! In the next chapter, I'm going to delve into the process of synthesis – what it is, and how it works.

Chapter 3 – What is synthesis?

In order to understand a synthesizer, it's important to understand the difference between a synthesizer and a more traditional musical instrument. As discussed in Chapter 1, sound is a vibration that travels through the air.

All non-electronic musical instruments physically create controlled vibrations in order to produce their tone. A guitar string produces a musical note when it's plucked by vibrating at a frequency defined by the length of the string, which is why a guitar's fret board allows the player to vary the length of a string. The sound of a flute is a column of air within the flute vibrating -and covering the holes of the flute varies the size of this column. Even a human voice singing a fixed tone is a product of the vocal cords vibrating at a fixed length and tension, driven by air pressure from the lungs.

Subtractive synthesizers, as musical instruments, also produce vibrations at specific frequencies. However, the mechanism is different. A hardware synthesizer uses a device called an oscillator. An oscillator generates an electronic vibration, according to a set waveform, at a set frequency. This vibration, once it's worked its way through the processing circuitry inside the synthesizer (all of which we'll cover in later chapters), gets picked up by the synthesizer's amplifier, which increases the volume of the signals. Once these signals are connected to an audio speaker (such as hi-fi speakers or a pair of headphones), the speakers output the signals as an audio sound by vibrating to match the signals coming out of the amplifier.

There are two ways modern synthesizers create their sound – hardware and software. A hardware synthesizer is one that generates and processes its sound using electronic circuitry, whereas a software synthesizer simulates the workings of a hardware synthesizer using computer code. There are some synthesizers that use physical pots and buttons, but simulate their inner workings with an on-board computer chip.

Because synthesis is a unique way to create sound, synthesizers possess their own particular sound palette. This varies from synthesizer to synthesizer and is a product of their circuitry and components (on a physical synthesizer) or a product of their code (on a computerised synthesizer). There is a chapter later in this book dedicated entirely to the perceived character of different synthesizers.

All sound design using synthesizers is through a two-part process:

1) The creation of sound
2) The manipulation of the sound created

Each synthesizer possesses common features, and you will learn how to effectively harness them in this book.

A note of caution - this book will teach you about traditional synthesizers, i.e. a synthesizer that creates and manipulates waveforms. How do you know if a synthesizer is traditional? It should have selectable waveforms and areas such as the ones you'll discover in this book. If a synthesizer has a bunch of presets for tuba, piano, choir and drums, it's sample-based. This means that tone generation is done through playing small recordings of sounds rather than through oscillators.

That's not to say that this book won't provide value if you primarily use a sample-based synthesizer, as sample-based synthesizers possess many features in common with traditional synthesizers, however this book is geared to those who wish to program synthesizers in a traditional sense, for example Moog and Roland's synthesizers, or the virtual synthesizers that come with software like Logic and Reason.

Exercises – Q&A

1) What does an oscillator do?
2) How does the signal from the oscillator become audible sound?
3) What is the two-part process of sound design on a synthesizer?

If you need any help, the answers are in Appendix A.

Chapter 4 – Getting started

Download, install and open Caustic using whichever computing device you've decided to use. It might open a demo track. Feel free to play it, but you'll be working from scratch! Next, create a new file by clicking on the three lines in the bottom left of Caustic:

Then, click on New:

Once your new file is open, click on the Machine Panel in the bottom left:

Press slot No. 1:

Add a SubSynth:

Click on your newly added SubSynth and you should be good to go:

19

If you're using a different DAW (Digital Audio Workstation, or music software), please follow that DAW's steps to open one of the subtractive synths detailed in the preface.

Exercises – Practice

1) If you found the instructions in this chapter difficult, repeat the process above! You'll need to get used to it for this book.

Chapter 5 – An Introduction to Caustic

Now you're all set up, let me explain what Caustic is and the reasons that Caustic is the most suitable tool with which to undertake this wonderful journey into synthesis.

You may have heard of Reason, Logic, or Ableton before – Caustic is similar, in that it is software that can be used to create music. It's certainly more limited than the above music software, however that merely makes the process of learning simpler and quicker – you don't have to put in lots of effort learning the software in order to be able to use it.

There are three reasons I've chosen Caustic as a platform to teach synthesis within this book:

1) Caustic can be used on most computing platforms – whether you're using a desktop PC, a tablet or smartphone.

2) It is very simple to use.

3) It's not as popular as the well-known music software out there. This makes it less likely that you, dear reader, have used it before. This is great because if you have used a synthesizer before, you will have to get out of your comfort zone and discard your preconceived working methods in order to adapt to Caustic's synthesizer – and therefore you will have to build a solid knowledge base from nothing!

The vast majority of the lessons within this book will take place on Caustic's in-built subtractive synthesizer, SubSynth. I've chosen SubSynth as it contains the vast majority of features that most synthesizers have. It's a basic, simple, functional synthesizer, and it doesn't sound that good by itself! This is exactly the sort of platform you should learn on, as a complex synthesizer with more bells and whistles will not only be harder to learn, but will give you instant, great-sounding results – without you ever truly learning *how* everything works.

Anyway, now you're all set up, and you've opened a SubSynth, it's time to take a closer look at the synth you will be using to create some sounds:

The different areas of the synth's layout are indicated by grey writing with a black background in the top left of the area. This, for example, is the volume envelope area:

These areas, marked with the black background in the top left (you see where it says Volume Envelope?), are the areas that I will refer to in these instructions. You should be able to find similar areas marked on your synthesizer, if you're using a different one.

Look again at SubSynth. Let's work our way through the different sections. I will systematically teach you the different functions of each section over the next chapters, one-by-one. Try to locate these areas on SubSynth – a full description of their function is available in Appendix B at the back of the book:

1) The patch section. This is unmarked, but is in the top-left under the SubSynth logo, and contains a box with the words *Select preset*.

2) Oscillator 1 and Oscillator 2 – these are below the patch section.

3) Bend – to the right of Oscillator 1.

4) Filter - to the right of the patch section.

5) LFO 1 and LFO 2 - to the right of the filter.

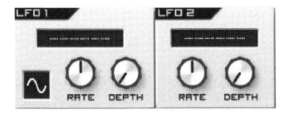

6) The Volume Envelope – above the keyboard, right of centre.

7) The Output – on the right, above the keyboard.

8) The keyboard section – along the bottom, it looks like a piano, you can't miss it!

As I stated earlier in Chapter 3, all sound generation with synthesizers uses using a two-part process:

1) The generation of sound

2) The manipulation of the sound generated

We can harness this two-part process to learn how to generate the sounds we want.

First things first, you'll notice that SubSynth says *Select preset* in the patch selector. Click on the floppy disk to the right of it to save the patch. Save it as *Init:*

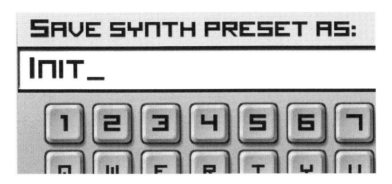

Init has a special meaning in the world of synthesis – it's short for *initial.* The idea behind an Initial patch is that it's a blank canvas to start from – a basic, no frills patch to start with that you can consistently build from. You always start from an Init patch when creating something new.

It's very possible that you're used to using pre-programmed patches, which, by their very nature, are programmed to sound good. However, you're starting from scratch here – which means that the sound experiments you undertake may not sound good by comparison. This is absolutely fine – it's only by going back to the drawing board that we can learn to extract consistent, well thought-out sounds from our synthesizer.

Now you're prepared, it's time for the next chapter, and your first step on your journey to sound alchemy! It's time to learn about the oscillators.

Exercises – Q&A

1) What is this section called?

2) What is this section called?

If you need any help, the answers are in Appendix A.

Chapter 6 – Single Oscillators

Now you're all set up, it's time to create some sounds. In this chapter, you will focus on a single oscillator of your synthesizer and the sound it creates.

Oscillator 1 should be set to the sine wave (i.e. it should look like the picture below). If it's not, click the waveform in the box until it looks like the below:

Now play a note on the keyboard at the bottom of the synthesizer.

I find it a smooth, round sound.

Now try playing a really low bass note and a few high notes. You can do this on Caustic by changing the octave of the keyboard using the Up and Down arrows to the right of the keyboard

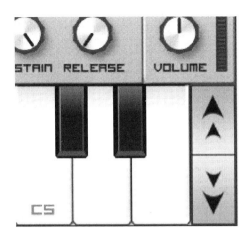

Press those arrows until you notice that C5 change to a C4 or C6. To play a low note, I'd suggest having that right C5 be a C3, and to play a high note, I'd suggest making that C5 a C7. If you can't hear any low notes, try turning your system up a bit or using better earphones! If all else fails, play higher notes until you at least hear *something*.

While playing these different notes, did you notice how the bass is booming, but the high notes are very delicate, in the sense that they could get drowned out very easily if there were other instruments playing alongside them? To find out why, let's get an oscilloscope. As you'll recall from Chapter 1, waveform is a property of sound. An oscilloscope is a machine that allows us to view and analyse the waveform that comes out.

In addition to an oscilloscope, we'll use an EQ analyzer. This will show us a lot of the audible audio spectrum, and we can use it to find out which frequencies are loud in a note and which frequencies are quiet.

31

Don't worry if you don't have an oscilloscope lying around - I'll show you the outputs in this book. Here's the oscilloscope's view of a sine wave:

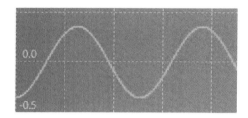

Notice something? The synthesizer outputs the same waveform as you selected by the oscillators. This very same waveform is moving the physical parts of your speakers in order to create the vibrations in the air that your ears can hear, just as described in Chapter 1. Traditional instruments, such as pianos and violins create highly complex waveforms. However, the wave you create on a synthesizer is exactly the wave that comes out of your speakers. That's the beauty of synthesis - it really is that direct. For clarity's sake, allow me to repeat the graphic illustrating the process that's occurring here:

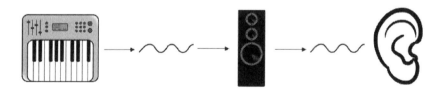

Let's have a look at the EQ analysis of our sine wave. Remember that lower frequencies are on the left, and higher frequencies are on the right:

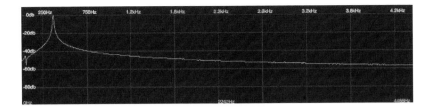

Do you see that peak? That's our sine wave. Do you see how it's very focused on the frequency that's playing? The sine wave isn't creating any frequencies above or below the note being played. This is quite unlike real-life sounds (for example, a human voice), where a sound will create a lot of different frequencies at the same time. For comparison, this is my voice through an EQ analyzer:

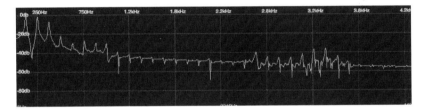

Now you have tested a sine wave, try a square wave by clicking on the waveform in oscillator 1 to find the wave that looks like a square. Play a note using the square wave. To me, it's a harsh, wooden sound:

Try a low note, a middle note and a high note (using the octave buttons where necessary), and take a moment to compare and contrast the sounds, thinking about what sort of sensation and emotion they create. We know how this will look on the oscilloscope, but let's have a look at our EQ analyzer:

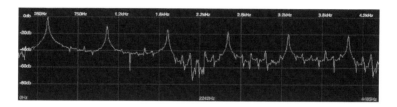

Notice that fuzz above the fundamental (in this case the lowest) frequency being played? These are harmonics and overtones. Harmonics are mathematical ratios of a fundamental frequency, and they are everything in music and sound. Overtones are additional frequencies above the fundamental that are not necessarily precisely mathematically proportional, but they add to the sound.

The sounds we love, from guitar strings to voices, are due to harmonic overtones. Even our Western musical scale (i.e. the keys on a piano) are designed to approximate parts of the harmonic series. The harmonic series works in a mathematical scale, from the first to the second, second to the third, etc. To find out more about the harmonic series, I recommend Harmony for Computer Musicians by Michael Hewitt (yes, we are related).

The square wave you just played contains harmonics, but only odd-numbered ones (i.e. 1st, 3rd, 5th, etc.). Did you notice that the square wave makes for a powerful bass note, but stands out a bit more when you play high notes with it? That's thanks to those lovely harmonics.

Now try a Triangle wave by clicking through the oscillator again until you find the triangular wave:

 Notice how it sounds like the square, but much more restrained? That's because just like the square wave, it only contains odd-numbered harmonics. The reason for this is that as the frequency of the harmonics increase, the amplitude (volume) of these harmonics decrease to a much higher degree than they would with a square wave. This is governed by the mathematics of the waveform produced. Here's the EQ analysis for comparison:

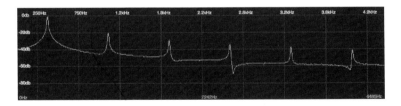

Now let's try the next one, a sawtooth:

I find this a harsh, clear, piercing sound. Did you notice how it struggled with the bass notes, but fared admirably at the top end? Let's find out why using an EQ analyzer:

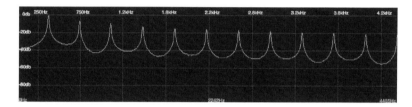

The sawtooth is harmonically rich, and whereas the square wave merely gave us odd harmonics, the sawtooth delivers all harmonics.

There's one more significant oscillator waveform to try - the Noise setting:

Once again, play some low, mid and high notes. Did you notice that regardless of the key, the sound is the same? That TV tuned to a dead channel sound? Let us look at the EQ analyzer again:

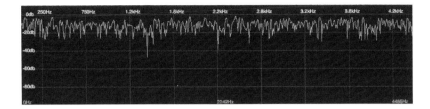

Have you spotted it? The Noise function gives you pretty much every frequency at the same time, to the same extent (the peaks and troughs vary quickly over time).

Now you have worked through each oscillator in this chapter, I'm going to leave you with my conclusions. Bear in mind some of it is my opinion as a musician, and you're welcome to disagree:

· The sine wave is the simplest waveform, containing no harmonics. It sounds smooth and gentle.

· The square wave is a fairly harsh, wooden sound, containing odd harmonics.

· The triangle wave has similar bass abilities to the sine, but with a limited degree of odd harmonics in addition.

· The sawtooth is a brash, harsh sound, with a lot of harmonics.

In the next chapter, you're going to continue learning about oscillators - this time, you're going to mix them together.

Exercises – Q&A

1) What are the five oscillators mentioned in this chapter?
2) Which oscillator has the most harmonic content?
3) Which oscillator is only active in odd-numbered harmonics?
4) Which oscillator gives you the same sound, regardless of which note you play on the keyboard?
5) Which oscillator sounds smooth?
6) Which oscillator sounds harsh?

If you need any help, the answers are in Appendix A.

Exercise – Practice

1) Apply your active listening skills to each of the oscillators. Eliminate distractions, just as you did in the active listening chapter. Play each oscillator, one at a time. Cycle through them and play them again, noting down in a notebook what you think of their sounds. You might want to think about texture, emotion, possible contexts, or even tracks where you've heard that kind of sound before.

Chapter 7 – Oscillator mixing & manipulation

Now you have a basic idea of how each oscillator sounds in isolation, in this chapter you're going to explore what happens when you mix them together. It would be a bit arduous to go through each combination, but you're going to work through a few combinations to highlight some important principles.

You will need to move your Mix dial (or your oscillator mixers if you have a different synthesizer) to the middle, so that each oscillator is mixed equally. If you have individual faders for your oscillators because you're using a different synthesizer, place them both at an equal level:

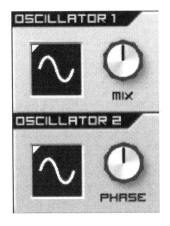

Put a sine wave on each of your oscillators, ensuring the oscillator mixer is mixing both oscillators equally. Now try to play a middling note. Not a lot happened, did it?

Key to this is the oscillator pitch - because not only can we output an oscillator pitch through pressing notes on our keyboard, but we can also manipulate that pitch at a note and microtone level, using the Semis and Cents pots respectively.

While holding this note, move your Semis pot on oscillator 2 one notch to the right if you're using a touchscreen this may require some delicate work:

This may sound unpleasant – this is because you're moving the frequency of oscillator 2 one semitone upwards – as if you were also playing the note above the note you're holding on the keyboard. Move the Semis pot another six notches to the right – making seven notches in total. That sounds a bit better, doesn't it? That's because you're now playing a Fifth chord while holding down a single note – as if you're playing notes E and B together on a guitar.

Switch both of your oscillators to sawtooths (HQ) and play a note. Then, turn the Cents dial to about 11pm and play a note again:

Hear the difference? Let's find out what's going on using the oscilloscope:

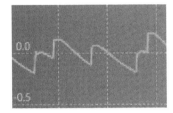

Look carefully at the oscilloscope output above. Do you see the smaller peaks in addition to the bigger peaks? These are sawtooth harmonics, and they're constructively and destructively interfering with each other.

Next, switch your Semis and Cents pots back to 12pm, and move the Phase pot to around 3pm:

What this does is set oscillator 2's waveform out of phase (or out of sync) with oscillator 1. Both waveforms peaking are visible on the oscilloscope:

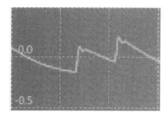

Using the Phase pot, we have altered the timing of the peaks and troughs of our waveforms to create even more interference! Whereas both our oscillators' waveforms used to peak and trough at the same time, now they do so at different times. To look at it another way, imagine we drop two stones into a pond which land at precisely the same time. All we're going to do by dropping the extra stone is create a bigger wave. However, if we drop one stone in very slightly after one another, the two are going to create differently-timed waves which interfere with one another. This also explains why the effect disappears when we set our Phase pot to precisely midday – because that puts our two waveforms back in synchronisation:

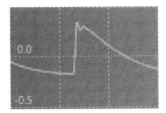

Now, it's time to move the Octave dial. This essentially plays the same note but at a different octave to your original tone. For the musically minded, an octave is the same note but lower or higher on your keyboard. For the scientifically minded, it's precisely half the frequency of the fundamental tone.

You'll have noticed a pot next to your oscillators called Bend:

This is designed to simulate an effect found on many synthesizers called Portamento. From the French word portmanteau describing a word that blends the sounds and meanings of two others (e.g. brunch), Portamento blends two tones together. Try turning Bend to about 1pm and playing some notes. Notice how they seem to glide up and down together? Now try it around 11am. Do you notice how the note seem to bend from the bottom, rather than the top? That's because you've moved the dial to the left of centre. Bend isn't immediately useful to us in the context of this book, but we'll keep it in our back pocket– so I'd suggest you turn Bend back to midday for the time being.

Next, turn the FM dial up. Notice how the sound seems to get a bit fatter? That's because FM stands for Frequency Modulation – what we have done is add some more harmonics by modulating the oscillator waveform, using frequencies already being output. Please note that if you're using a different synthesizer to Caustic's SubSynth, you may get drastically different results from enabling FM – this is often because many FM-enabled synthesizers allow you to specify your modulation frequency.

If you switch it to AM, you are modulating the sound through a technique called Amplitude Modulation, which adds harmonics to the signal by using the synthesizer's amplitude to modulate the sound. PM also exists as a function – this uses the synthesizer's amplitude to change the phase of the oscillator, thereby adding harmonics, like so:

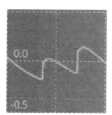

AM and PM are not hugely important to your overall journey in comparison to the more important features of the synthesizer, so on that basis, we will move on to the more important elements of the synthesizer for our next stage in the journey.

For the next chapter, you can retain this synthesizer patch that you have created and move on to the next stage in the journey – the filter. If you're returning to this book later, please use the floppy disk button to Save your patch. It should look like this:

Just select a memorable patch name, and save it. All software synthesizers should possess a similar function. If you happen to be using a hardware synthesizer, you could even go old-school and use a patch sheet – although taking a photo will more than suffice.

In this chapter, you have worked on both oscillators, trying out their different functions and waveforms, testing how they combine to create different sounds. In the next chapter, you will be moving on to the filter function of the SubSynth synthesizer.

Exercises – Q&A

1) What does the semis pot do?

2) What does the octave pot do?

3) What does the cents pot do?

4) What does the Bend pot do?

5) If you wanted to set two oscillators out of sync with each other, so that the peaks and troughs of the waveforms land in different places relation to each other, how would you do this?

If you need any help, the answers are in <u>Appendix A</u>.

Exercises – Practice

1) Try further combinations of oscillator mixes using an active listening approach, noting the ones you enjoy.
2) Try selecting two identical waveforms on both oscillators and altering the pitch controls to hear the difference.

Chapter 8 – Filters

In this chapter, you're going to use SubSynth's filter to manipulate the oscillators' output.

Before you start using the filter on the synthesizer, it's important to understand what a filter is, and how it works. Filters are used in a wide variety of electronic devices, and are used to remove unwanted parts from any type of signal:

Filters can be found everywhere. Your broadband equipment uses filters to block out unwanted noise on the phone line. Your speakers use filters to decide which audio signals to send to which parts of the speaker. Your analogue radio uses filters – when you tune it, you're merely filtering out all the frequencies you *don't* want it to tune to.

There are three primary types of filter used in audio – low-pass, high-pass, and band-pass. By pass, it means that it allows that type of signal through. Low-pass filters allow low frequencies (i.e. low notes) through, high-pass filters allow high frequencies through, and band-pass filters allow a band of your choosing through. It's best to illustrate this using your synthesizer, so set up your patch as below –

an Init patch with two sawtooths, but with Cents dialed back to 11am:

Now, click once on the display part of the filter, in order to select LowPass:

Play a note – it should sound like a normal, harsh, sawtooth. This is what the EQ analyzer looked like when you did this:

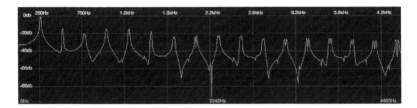

Now, bring the cutoff down to the bottom, and play the note again. Sounds like the note is playing from behind a wall, doesn't it? This is the EQ analyzer's take on it:

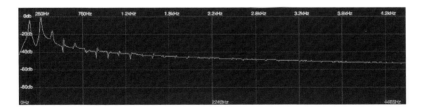

As you can see, it's letting the low frequencies (on the far left of the picture) *pass through* and suppressing the higher frequencies.

If you switch your filter to high-pass and move cutoff all the way to the top, you'll observe a similar effect with high frequencies, whereby your low frequencies are suppressed (look at the downward curve in the middle of the picture):

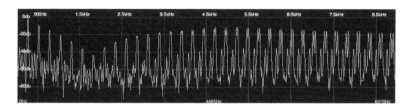

Next, switch the filter to Bandpass. Hold down a note, and then move the cutoff up and down. Do you notice that it's allowing certain frequencies through depending on where you move the filter? That's because it's allowing a band in the middle of your frequency range through – and where that band is depends on where you select using the filter.

If you're using Caustic's SubSynth – you'll notice three more filters – Inv. LP, Inv. BP and Inv. HP. You may notice that these seem to have the opposite effect on the sound. Don't worry about these for the time being – they're a more advanced feature that we'll get to in a later chapter.

In addition to cutoff, you'll have noticed a feature called res. This means resonance. This comes from an artifact on analogue filters, whereby the frequency you selected to cut off at is actually amplified (i.e. increases in volume) – this increase in volume around the cutoff

50

frequency adds character to your sound – from a bit of added 'bite' when used sparingly to a squeal when a lot of resonance is added.

To hear this, put your filter back to Low Pass, turn your resonance all the way up, and hold down a note while moving the cutoff up and down. Can you hear that harmonic-sounding whistle? That's resonance, amplifying one of your harmonics. It's subtle, but you can see the effect on the EQ analyzer at around 1.8kHz (look just left of centre):

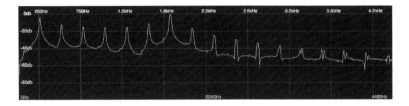

Next, find the Track pot, and turn it all the way up, and set a Low Pass filter to halfway:

Play some lower notes (changing the octave on your keyboard if required) and some higher ones. Did you notice any difference? The Track function selectively alters your filter values based on the notes playing, so that higher notes are filtered less, and lower notes are filtered more. This is parameter is particularly used in melodies and sequences that utilise both lower notes and higher notes – by filtering the higher notes to a lesser degree, it highlights them to the listener, making the melody sound more expressive.

In this chapter, we have used the filter to filter out the frequencies we don't want and used the EQ analyzer to interpret scientifically what the filter is doing.

There's no doubt that you will have noticed four pots within your filter:

These are for your filter envelope – and envelopes are the subject of the next chapter.

Exercises – Q&A

1) What are the three primary types of filter used in audio?

2) What frequencies get let through if you use a high-pass filter?

3) What does Resonance do?

4) What does Track do?

If you need any help, the answers are in Appendix A.

Exercises - Practice

1) Use different combinations of oscillators and oscillator pitches to create various sounds, and then use the filter to establish what effect the filter has on various combinations. For example, try sine wave oscillators. Now compare these to the effect of using a sawtooth oscillator with a Noise oscillator. Remember to actively listen throughout.

2) Use the filter on various oscillator setups to create different effects, thinking about where you might have heard this kind of filtering in action in music you've heard.

Chapter 9 – Envelopes

One of the most important elements of a musical note is how it changes over time when it's played.

Envelope is the setting on a synthesizer that not only allows you to control the duration of the sound, but how quickly it begins, how quickly it declines from its peak volume, how loud it is at its peak, and how long it lasts after you stop playing the note.

This is the volume envelope section on your SubSynth. It has four pots – Attack, Decay, Sustain and Release. So far, you've been using the synthesizer controls to alter the timbre of your sound. The volume envelope section is there to enable you to control the dynamics of your sound over time.

Often known as an ADSR envelope, the envelope is commonly visualised using the below graphic:

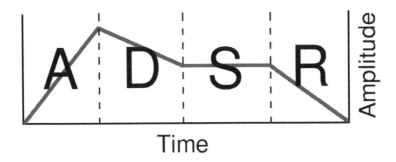

Don't worry if that drawing doesn't make sense to you yet. Here's the four components of it broken down by control:

· Attack controls how long it takes for the note to get to full volume after the note has been pressed. The notes you've been playing in the exercises so far reach full volume immediately because the attack is set as low as possible.

· Decay controls how quickly the note's volume transitions to the level set by the...

· Sustain – which controls the volume of the sound once the Attack and Decay phases have elapsed.

· Release governs how long it takes for the note to stop sounding after the key is released.

For example, think of a violin. This has a fairly fast Attack because the note begins quickly, a quick decay (as it transitions to the

Sustain level quickly), a high Sustain level (because continuing to play the note keeps the note sustained at the same level), and a fast Release.

On the other hand, a snare drum hit has a very fast attack, a very fast Decay, no Sustain (because holding the stick against the drum after hitting it has little to no effect) and a fairly slow Release (as the sound dissipates).

To look at it another way, let's follow the journey of a single note in the graphic above. Let's pretend that it corresponds to a key press lasting exactly one second. Here's its timeline:

1) The note goes from zero volume to its peak volume (Attack).
2) It then declines in volume slightly (Decay).
3) It holds the level of volume it's declined to while the note is held down (Sustain).
4) The note is released, and the sound tapers away (Release).

People who are new to synthesis can often get confused as to why Decay comes before Sustain, or what the difference is between Decay and Release. Just think of it in terms of the three stages of pressing a synthesizer note:

1) The note gets pressed down – Attack and Decay decide what happens to the volume of the sound.
2) The note gets held down – the Sustain level decides the volume of note for this stage.

3) The note gets released – Release now decides what happens to the volume of the note.

It's time to gain some experience in using the volume envelope. Create a patch as below:

Press a note. It starts and ends when your note press starts and ends.

Now move the Attack up to midday and play a note:

Did you notice how the note took longer to start sounding?

Now move your Sustain down to about 3pm and hold down a note:

Notice that the note lowers in volume suddenly, but doesn't disappear entirely? That's because the Sustain level is set low. This means that the note is taking time to rise to its peak, but is subsequently dropping down to the low Sustain level once it has peaked.

You can make this drop sound slightly more natural by increasing the Decay to midday:

However, we're best off illustrating the effect of envelopes using two contrasting examples. Firstly, set your envelope as shown below and play some notes:

Hear how they sound like tiny little blips?

Now set your Volume envelope like this, and play some notes again:

Do you hear how the notes collide and harmonise with each other after you've released the key? That's because your Release is set to a high level.

Now let's experiment a little bit more. Drag the sidebar upwards to bring yourself to Caustic's sequencer:

If you're using your own DAW/synth, use the piano roll or whatever equipment you have to hand to program a 16-step sequence. If you're not musically experienced, feel free to copy my sequence by tapping/clicking the below notes into the piano roll to match my pattern:

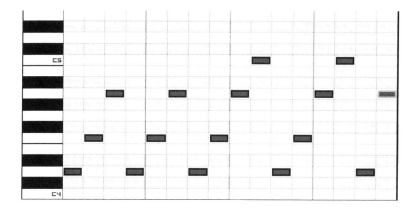

Now press Play, and then scroll back up to SubSynth.

Now experiment with the Volume envelope. As an example, keep the Attack and Decay low, the Sustain around midday and alter the Release pot. Get a feel for the tension and release that can be created by changing the Release amount as the sequence plays.

If you like, feel free to add a filter and alter the cutoff. You could even add an additional oscillator, move Cents slightly and move oscillator 2's octave around. One of my favourite aspects of synthesis is to let a sequence run and alter the parameters to find out what sounds can be created. Here's a setup that I felt sounded good for the sequence:

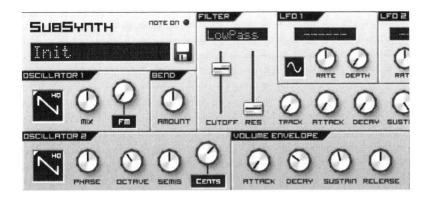

Once you've found a setup that you feel sounds good, save it. If you didn't, feel free to copy mine above and save it using a memorable name (just use the floppy disk next to the patch name).

In this chapter, we have found out what an envelope is and how it effects the volume of your sound. In the next chapter, we'll explore filter envelopes – envelopes that govern the filter rather than the note volume.

Exercises – Q&A

1) Which part of the envelope controls how long the note sounds for after the note is no longer being played?

2) Which part of the envelope controls how quickly the note initially takes to reach peak volume?

3) Which part of the envelope controls how loud a note is while the note is being held?

4) Which part of the envelope controls how long a note takes to reach the level set by Sustain?

If you need any help, the answers are in <u>Appendix A</u>.

Exercises – Practice

1) Use the oscillators to create a sound you find interesting. Now use the envelopes to create long, sweeping notes, and then use the envelopes to create short blips.

2) Use your active listening skills to find different combinations of oscillators and envelope setups, making a mental note of the different musical effects that you could possibly create using a combination of these two parameters.

Chapter 10 – Filter Envelopes

In this chapter, you will look at how filter envelopes interact with the filter and how you can use these to create interesting, novel sounds.

Using the patch you created that you felt sounded good (or mine at the end of the previous chapter), play a few notes, setting the filter to LowPass and moving the filter up and down. When you've finished leave the filter at about three quarters of the way up – this is because you will use this setting to test the filter envelopes:

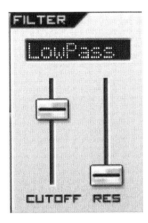

The four buttons to the right of Track are your filter envelopes.

Do you recall the volume envelope from the last chapter?

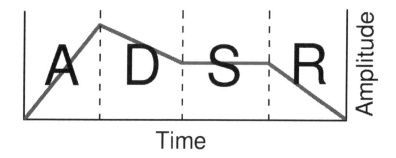

The filter envelope applies precisely the same principle, but rather than modify the amplitude (or volume) of the notes, it modifies the extent to which the notes are filtered.

To demonstrate an example, move the filter envelope Attack to around 10 o'clock, and play a few notes:

Do you notice how the notes seem to curl into the sound, rather than sound immediately? This is because the filter is applied slowly.

The opposite effect can also be achieved. On many synthesizers, the filter envelopes start around midnight (no effect) and can be increased or decreased. However, Caustic's SubSynth achieves this effect through *inverting* the filter. This means that moving the cutoff down on a low pass filter actually filters fewer frequencies, rather than more.

Try retaining your settings, but changing the filter to Inv. LP:

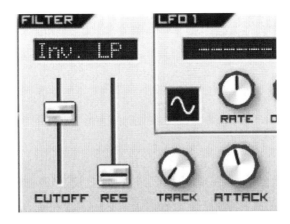

Do you notice how the sound seems to pop out? This is because the filter is open at the start of the note, but then it gets closed down quickly.

Try changing your volume envelope's Decay and Sustain to full (around 5 o'clock), and then turning your filter envelope's Decay to around 1pm with the sustain at 7pm. Hold down a note:

Do you notice how the note seems to open, then close again? This is because the volume envelope's Sustain holds the note, while the filter envelope's Decay setting applies the filter and then removes it as it runs through the envelope you've selected. This is one of the most important elements of synthesis – the way that the volume envelope interacts with the filter envelope.

If you bring your filter envelope release and sustain down to 7 o'clock, and play a note, the note seems to sound twice:

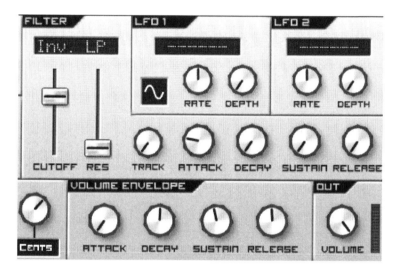

To understand what's happening here, look at both envelopes and imagine them acting upon a note at the same time. Can you work it out? The answer is below:

The reason the note seems to sound twice is because the filter envelope's release and sustain setting is so low, the filter envelope releases before the volume envelope states that the note should elapse. In other words, the filter envelope ceases to act upon the note, but the note's still going!

The above example is a way you can encounter difficulties with a filter envelope, but a thorough understanding of the fundamentals of filter envelopes will mean you know precisely what to do when these difficulties occur.

Filter envelopes can be extremely powerful. For example, mimic this setting:

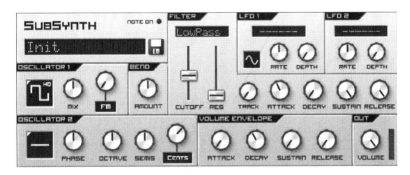

Now play some bass notes. Do you recognise something familiar in that bass sound? This is a synthesizer patch used in urban music for at least 20 years – and the bass you are playing can be found across Garage, House and the predecessor to the wobble bass found in Dubstep music.

In this chapter, you have learned about filter envelopes and learned how they interact with your Volume envelope to create sounds full of dynamism and character.

What if the controls we are using could be automated across time? So that they would work independently of the notes we played?

As I'm sure you've surmised, this forms the content of our next chapter: LFOs.

Exercises – Q&A

1) To apply the filter slowly to the sound, what control would you alter?

2) To create precisely the opposite effect, applying the filter to the sound quickly, what would you do?

3) If you were using a synthesizer without an inverted filter available, and you wanted an inverted filter effect, what would you do?

If you need any help, the answers are in <u>Appendix A</u>.

Exercises – Practice

1) Practise using the filter envelopes in conjunction with the volume envelopes. Try to get the setup wrong, so that you can't hear anything – and then rescue it!

2) Practise using the filter envelopes with both the normal filter settings and the inverted filter settings.

3) Practise using the envelopes to create aggressive, sharp sounds and contrasting slow, growing sounds. By the end of the practice, you should be able to switch between the two with ease.

Chapter 11 – LFOs

In this chapter, we're going to approach the LFO function and its implications for your music.

Thanks to the understanding of oscillators that you've gleaned from Chapters 2 & 3, you will hopefully be able to broach the subject matter of LFOs without too much difficulty.

LFO stands for Low Frequency Oscillator. This stems from a moment of engineering genius, wherein analogue synthesizer engineers added another oscillator, however instead of this being an audible oscillator, it was an oscillator that simply effected the other components of the synthesizer. In these synthesizers, the LFO oscillators tended to operate at rates below 20Hz – too low a frequency to form an audible tone.

LFOs, despite being oscillators, are not designed to be directly audible – instead, they are designed to manipulate signals that already exist in the sound.

For example, start from your Init patch and create two sawtooth oscillators. Use the Semis pot to place oscillator 2 7 semitones above oscillator 1 and move Cents to about 2pm. Then, add a LowPass filter. Should you require assistance with this, you can use the image below for reference:

Play a tone – you should hear a pure, sonorous chord. If you don't, make sure Semis is exactly 7 semitones above midday, as this creates a fifth chord.

Try playing Notes C and Eb together – if you're musically inexperienced, that's these ones:

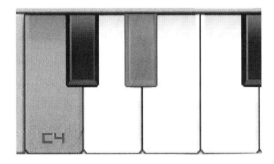

You should hear a pretty pleasant tone.

Now, move up to LFO 1, and select a sine wave LFO, using the same technique you would use to select an oscillator. Use the control panel to send it to Osc 1 & 2. Move the rate pot to about 2:30 and the depth to about 9:30pm:

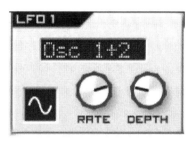

Notice the difference? The tone seems to be vibrating. Try holding down the above chord and turning the depth all the way up. Do you notice how additional depth seems to increase the extent to which the sound wobbles? This is because the LFO is sending a signal directly to the oscillators, forcing them to vary their tone according to the oscillator waveform.

The two pots on the LFO perform very simple functions – the Rate changes the speed at which the LFO oscillates (i.e. vibrates). Depth changes the extent to which the LFO affects its destination – more depth means more effect.

Now try a little challenge. I want you to turn the Filter into an Inverted LP filter, filter cutoff down to halfway, and use both the volume envelope and the filter envelope to give the patch a fairly sharp envelope – one that's bright at the start but closes quickly, with a bit of Release in the volume envelope left over. I want it to almost sound like the kind of envelope a piano would have.

Let's see how you did – this is what I came up with:

Now, create some notes. Scroll down to your sequencer and distribute 3-6 of those chords that you played earlier in a manner that makes rhythmic sense across the bar. Here's my example:

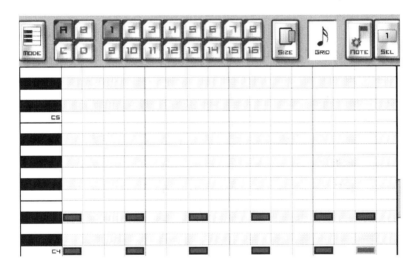

Of course, if you're musically experienced, feel free to create your own rhythmic chord sequence of a similar rhythm to mine.

Press play, and then alter the filter cutoff and resonance. Find a sweet spot that you like. Can you guess what you're doing next?

Send LFO 2 to the cutoff. Turn the depth up and bring the rate down:

As you can hear, you've automated the cutoff on your filter. You will notice that if you move the filter around, the LFO moves with it – if you completely open up the cutoff, the LFO only seems to work some of the time. This is because the LFO modifies your existing values. And when, for example, the LFO tries to push the filter beyond its limits – or higher than it can possibly go anyway, it stops having an effect on the sound.

Hopefully, this is starting to sound good. Now, it's time to apply some of what you've learned from previous chapters. Play with your envelopes, your filters (including different filter types), and even throw in a couple of high notes into the sequencer, turning up the Track pot on the filter to emphasise them. Have fun trying to add some drama and tension to your sequence. Once again, the volume envelope is my go-to place for this, especially the Decay and Release pots. My hope is that you've had enough practice and gained enough knowledge using this book that even if you've tried to program a synthesizer in the past, you're now experimenting from a place of knowledge and understanding of the different functions of the synthesizer and how they affect your signal.

Exercises – Q&A

1) What does LFO stand for?

2) What's the difference between a normal oscillator and an LFO?

3) What does the Rate pot do?

4) What does the Depth pot do?

If you need any help, the answers are in <u>Appendix A</u>.

Exercises – Practice

1) Try routing your LFO to different destinations, varying the rate and depth to see how they affect your sound.
2) Try adding another LFO on LFO 2, routing them both to the same destination, and listen to the interaction between them.

Next, we're going to touch on a seemingly small but very important concept – polyphony.

Chapter 12 – Polyphony

Polyphony is a measure of how many notes your synthesizer can play at the same time. Within the world of analogue hardware synthesizers, polyphony is deeply embedded within the architecture, as it is restricted by the electronics of the device – this is because the tones are played by physical oscillators that can each only play a tone at a time. There tend to be three types of synthesizer polyphony, especially in hardware synthesis:

1) Monophonic – a monophonic synthesizer can only play one note at a time

2) Polyphonic – a polyphonic synthesizer can play more than one note at a time

3) Paraphonic – this is something you'll only really find in the hardware synthesizer world. This is where the synthesizer can play more than one note at the same time, but all the notes are forced through the same circuitry. So, for example, even though your first note would trigger the filter envelope, an additional note played would not.

In the software synthesis world, polyphony is rarely restricted.

You'll notice the polyphony setting on SubSynth down in the bottom-left, near the keyboard:

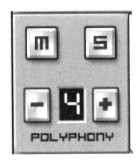

Try using the − button to turn it down to 2, then press 3 keys at once. It's hard to spot, but you'll notice that your 2 last notes will sound − this is called last-note priority.

However, the effect of polyphony is at its most pronounced when polyphony is reduced to 1. In effect, you're emulating a monophonic (restricted to one note at a time) synthesizer.

Try playing the keyboard with your polyphony turned down to 1:

This is where the beauty of monophonic synthesis comes into play. You'll notice that when you play a note, and while holding that note, play the next one, that the synthesizer moves smoothly to that next tone. This makes it perfect for playing synth leads − for an example, listen to *Any Colour You Like* by *Pink Floyd* − one of the finest examples of a monophonic synth lead around.

In fact, in spite that it comes across as a restriction, monophonic synthesis is responsible for some of the most prevalent motifs in contemporary music – including the Acid basslines produced by the monophonic Roland 303 (found in all manner of electronic music, especially Acid House) or the funky, expressive Minimoog basslines found in Parliament Funkadelic's work and its offshoots, including a lot of West Coast hip hop.

Now we have covered all the features of the SubSynth, it's time to get started on some more advanced chapters that you can immediately apply to your music production.

Exercises – Q&A

1) What does monophonic mean?

2) What does polyphonic mean?

3) How would you turn SubSynth into a monophonic synthesizer on Caustic?

If you need any help, the answers are in Appendix A.

Exercises – Practice

1) Turn SubSynth polyphony down to 1 and create a wonderful monophonic lead.

Chapter 13 – Effects

Whilst the next few chapters are not precisely about directly programming a synthesizer, it's such an important aspect of making synthesizers sound good, to leave it out would be to deprive you, dear reader, of a lot of insight.

There are a huge number of audio effects out there, each of which alter your sound in different pleasant (or unpleasant!) ways. In this chapter, we're going to learn the most fundamental, important effects. They are:

· Delay
· Reverb
· Chorus
· Flanger
· Phaser
· Compressor
· Limiter
· Parametric EQ

They can be grouped into categories:

· Delay effects - Reverb and Delay - These work by layering copies of the sound over the original sound at different time intervals, making your sound appear to echo or loop, after the initial sound has elapsed.

79

· Modulation effects - Chorus, Flanger, Phaser - these work by layering copies of the sound over the original sound at long time intervals, making your sound appear to echo or loop over itself.

· Compression effects - Compressor and Limiter - these work by assessing the loudness of the incoming sound and changing the loudness of the output depending on the settings.

· Equalization - Parametric EQ - this works by letting you selectively increase or decrease certain frequencies within your sound.

To explore your effects, create a patch that will serve to highlight them well. Load your Init patch, then use a sawtooth wave on oscillators 1 and 2, and then add an Inv. LP filter with a bit of resonance. I suggest you increase the attack on the filter envelope to about 10pm to create that bit of bite that your patch will need, and then increase the filter's Track to its fullest extent. Then, add a slow LFO and send it to the filter cutoff. Finally, move the Semis on oscillator 2 up 7 semitones to create a natural fifth chord.

Hopefully you were able to follow my instructions without issue, but if you were unsure, I'd suggest copying these settings:

Next, add in a quick sequence. I'd go for something in minor chords, with a few high notes peppered in. Copy mine if you want – notice how I've dragged the keyboard an octave down and my starting note is C3 – making my lowest notes lower, emphasising the high notes. You can drag the keyboard down by physically dragging the keyboard on the piano roll, using your finger or mouse:

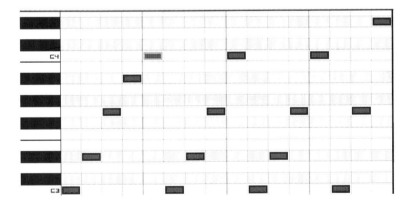

Play your sequence. You should hear the LFO modulating the filter as it goes – already fundamentally creating a usable sound.

Once you're on your sequencer, scroll down again and you should find this screen:

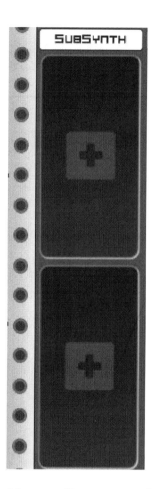

This is where you can add your effects. Press the +, and then add a Delay. Then, once you've completed the exercises, move on immediately to the next chapter!

Exercises – Q&A

1) Which types of effects involve creating copies of your sound?

2) Which type of effects alter the loudness of your sound?

3) Which type of effect involves creating copies of your sound that are timed close enough to your original that you can't distinguish the copies from the original?

4) What type of effect lets you increase or decrease the volume of your choice of frequency?

If you need any help, the answers are in <u>Appendix A</u>.

Chapter 14 - Delay Effects

Having added a Delay, you should immediately be able to hear the effect. What's happening is that the Delay is repeating copies of your sound at progressively lower volumes. Can you hear the interaction between your filter LFO and the delay? The way that the less filtered notes seem to linger in the sound when your LFO closes the filter? There are four functions on Caustic's delay, which can be found on most stereo delays (bear in mind the big red X is a delete button):

· Time. This governs how long a sound will be captured and repeated. You'll notice that if you move the Time pot all the way to the right, it captures a lot of the bar to repeat back to you. If you move it all the way to the left, you'll notice that it actually changes how the music sounds – because it's repeating extremely short snippets of sound straight back to you. Have some fun altering the time here – the rhythmic interaction of your sound with your delay is one of my favourite parameters when producing a sound!

· Feedback. Written as F.Back here, this governs how quickly (or slowly) the volume of each subsequent repetition is reduced. You'll notice that if you turn this all the way to the left, it seems to reduce the effect of the delay. If you turn it all the way to the right, you should notice the sound starts to build – this is because the delay is at the point where the amount of volume being reduced by each delay is less than the volume of delays being played on top. Be careful – this is literally a feedback loop! While Caustic kindly limits the volume of the delay feedback, I've come close to destroying speakers thanks to errant feedback loops in the past. Should you encounter a feedback loop in the wild, don't panic! Just bring the Feedback down – this soon clears out the delays layering upon each other.

· Wet. Also known as Wet/Dry, this simply governs how much of an effect your delay has. To make it easier, think of two signals – one is the signal affected by the Delay (wet), one is the signal not affected by the Delay (dry). By using the Wet pot you're simply choosing the extent to which each signal is mixed.

· Delay Type. The graphic down in the bottom governs how your delay is spread across your speakers. There are three main options. The first is the default (shown above), which is Mono. This means that the Delay sounds the same out of both your left and right speakers. If you click the Delay type, you'll find that it becomes this:

This effectively splits your delay into two, using one speaker's delay to affect the other. If you're not using headphones or stereo speakers to listen to the effect, I highly recommend you do so – it's a fantastic sound. Try listening to the different effects that you can achieve by modulating the time, from long, bouncing, enveloping effects using medium-long time parameters to effectively widening the sound by using an extremely short time parameter.

Once you've found a delay you're happy with, it's time to add some Reverb!

Click the + below your Delay:

Choose a Reverb:

Reverb

You will now be presented with the Reverb's controls:

Turn the Wet to midday or so, and you should hear a quiet amount of echo on the sequence you're playing – as if the sound is being played in an empty bathroom.

Reverb, while being one of the most used effects in music, is also very difficult to get right. It's meant to simulate sound echoing in a large, reflective room. Digital reverbs, be it hardware or software, use a complex set of algorithms to simulate this effect.

In order to experiment with your Reverb unit, you should first change your Delay's Wet to 7pm (i.e. as far to the left as it can go) to create a dry signal:

You'll see five controls on the Reverb unit. As the Reverb is intended to simulate a reverberant room, the controls are designed to alter the parameters of this room. This is what they do:

· Room controls the size of the room. If you move this back and forth, you'll find that moving it further to the right, thereby creating a bigger room, creates a larger reverb, and moving it to the left makes the room sound smaller – or non-existent at its furthest left setting.

· Damp simulates the sound absorption capacity of the walls of the simulated room. To test this, make the room as big as possible (by turning the pot all the way to the right) and then alter the Damp values. You'll find that turning the Damp all the way to the right makes the room's materials highly absorbent, so that very little reverb can be heard. Turning the Damp all the way to the left makes the room highly reflective, making the reverb sound big. Crudely, Damp acts as a low-pass filter on the reverberated signal; sound echoes well in a tiled bathroom with lots of reflective surfaces but

88

echoes poorly in a carpeted room with lots of absorbent material on the wall.

· Delay controls how long a delay is placed upon the echoes before they are mixed with the output. You'll find that a setting at seven o'clock makes the echoes arrive far sooner than a setting at five-o-clock. With this parameter, you're essentially controlling the distance of the sound from the reflective source.

· Width doesn't necessarily simulate a room, but it does control how much difference there is between the left and the right speaker – i.e. the stereo width of the reflections. A higher setting will create a more enveloping sound.

· Wet is precisely the same as it is on the Delay function – it controls how much signal is affected, and how much passes through 'Dry'.

Experiment with the various settings on the Reverb unit, creating small rooms and big rooms. When you're satisfied, turn the Wet up on the delay and have another attempt at changing the parameters of your SubSynth while a sequence is playing. Hopefully the knowledge you've gleaned from previous chapters makes it easier for you to choose which parameters to modulate on the synthesizer correctly. With enough practice, modulating these synthesizer parameters will be a controlled, educated process.

Before we move on to the next chapter, it's worth noting that the sequence of your effects matter. Currently, your Delay unit is routed into your Reverb unit. This means that your whole signal, including your Delays get affected by the Reverb unit. You can glean a different result if you reverse the order of the two – because your reverberated signal will be delayed, as opposed to the opposite. In the next chapter, we're going to put together all the knowledge we have gleaned so far to start recreating our own patches.

Finally, if you plan to take a break before continuing with the next chapter, I suggest you save your Caustic file. Just click on the button with the three lines at the left of Caustic's bottom bar:

Then click on Save and give your file a name.

Exercises – Q&A

1) Why can you hear less filtered notes overlaying more filtered notes when you've got the Delay running?

2) What does the Time parameter on the Delay function do?

3) What does feedback do?

4) Why does the sound seem to build if you move the feedback dial all the way to the right?

5) Why can't you hear your original sound if you move Wet/Dry all the way to Wet?

6) Why did I suggest you turn your Delay effect all the way to Dry before adding the reverb?

7) Why is the Room control called Room?

8) What does Delay do on a Reverb unit?

9) Why would you want to vary the width of the Reverb?

10) If you have multiple effects units on one signal (e.g. a Reverb and a Delay), why does their order matter?

If you need any help, the answers are in Appendix A.

Exercises – Practice

1) Try routing your signal through to the Reverb before the Delay. Make a mental note of the effect it has on the sound.

Before we move to the next chapter, use the Red X on Reverb and Delay units to remove them both:

Chapter 15 - Modulation Effects

Remove any effects that are currently on your sequence and add a Chorus:

Play your sequence. Do you notice how the sound is a lot thicker? How it sounds like it's moving and shimmering?

This is an effect that goes back to the chapter on multiple oscillators. Do you remember how varying Cents slightly would make your sound shimmer, like the effect you can hear now? That's because, just like when altering Cents, two similar sound waves, offset slightly using pitch or time, will constructively and destructively interfere with each other.

When exploring oscillators, we set the frequency of two Sawtooth waves slightly apart to create this interference:

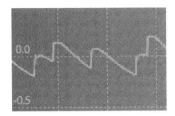

Instead of changing the pitch of one of the sound waves, the Chorus creates an identical copy of your sound and delays it– usually by between 20 and 50 milliseconds. There's a good reason for this timing, which we'll get to later.

To paraphrase, when using a Chorus, we modulate time to create the interference we want.

This effect can be found in nature – try striking a table repeatedly with one pen. Listen actively to the sound. Then try two pens at the same time. If you listen carefully, you might hear a Chorus effect, varying with each strike. Because of the slight time delay between when your left-handed pen and right-handed pen hits the table, a natural chorusing effect occurs.

Your Chorus has five main parameters:

· Depth
· Rate
· Delay
· Wet
· Waveform

te and Waveform should be eerily familiar to you. That is
‸use a Chorus uses an LFO, just like the LFO in SubSynth.
Whereas in SubSynth, your LFO controlled the part of the
synthesizer it was assigned to (for example, the filter), in the Chorus
the LFO controls the Chorus' in-built parameters.

· Depth controls the amount of LFO applied to your signal, which
transpires as how much of your signal is affected by the Chorus.

· Rate controls the rate of the LFO (usually up to roughly 10Hz, or 10
loops of the LFO per second)

· Waveform controls the waveform that the LFO uses

· Delay controls the time delay between your original audio signal
and its copy

· Wet is a control you already know from Reverb and Delay units – it
mixes your affected and unaffected signals together

Let's explore these controls with your sequence playing.

Firstly, bring your Delay and Rate pots all the way to 7pm (at the far
left). Do you notice how your signal almost sounds fattened? This is
because the Delay is so short, the sound waves have very little
opportunity to interfere with one another:

However, if you move the Rate up to 5pm (at the far right):

You'll find that the effect is far more pronounced. This is because even though the LFO's depth hasn't increased its grip on the effect, the sheer rate of the LFO's oscillation means that more waveform interference occurs.

For experiment's sake, move both your Depth and Rate to midday, and move your Delay all the way to the right at 5pm:

You'll notice that you can almost hear two copies of the sound. This is because the delay is now long enough that the amount of interference starts to reduce – and your brain no longer confuses the two copies of audio it hears as being from a single source.

This is the beauty of Chorus – it not only exploits the nature of sound waves, but exploits the brain's perception of them:

· Two identical sounds less than 10ms apart will be perceived as a single, normal sound
· Two identical sounds 10-50ms apart will be perceived as two independent sounds, but integrated into one altered sound
· Two identical sounds <50ms apart will be perceived as two independent, unintegrated sounds

Finally, turn your Depth to full, but alter your LFO waveform. I'm not going to discuss all the different LFO settings (as you should have an idea by now of what they do), but you will notice that a normal LFO:

Has far lesser an effect than a stereo LFO, which modulates the sound across both speakers differently:

This is because when you're looking for waveform interference between two signals, you'd be foolish to forget that your speakers are both separate signal paths – and can also be used to create interference.

We've gone into depth as to how a chorus works. The next two effects, Flanger and Phaser work in similar ways, which is why they're called modulation effects. Because we understand the basics of modulation effects, we'll work briefly with these two to get a feel for the effect they have on sound.

Remove your Chorus, and select a Flanger:

Play your sequence. You might notice that it sounds very similar to the Chorus. This is because the Flanger uses similar tricks to the Chorus to create its audial illusion. The Chorus specifically splits your audio signal into two identical copies, one of which is delayed. However, the Flanger varies the amount it's delayed by over time, and then moves this delay time back and forth – creating that long, characteristic sweeping sound you hear.

The controls on the Flanger are similar to the Chorus – the LFO Depth, Rate and Waveform. However, the Flanger also has the ability to pump the audio signal back into itself, thereby increasing the degree of effect. The F.Back (meaning Feedback) pot controls the extent to which this occurs. If you move the F.Back pot to 7pm (at the far left), you'll notice very little effect on your signal:

Whereas if you move your Feedback all the way to 5pm (at the far right), you'll notice that the peaks of your Flanged sound are quite loud and harsh:

To complete the triplet of modulation effects, remove the Flanger and add a Phaser in its place:

You'll notice that the audio played through the Phaser seems, once again, to shimmer, but in a different way to the Flanger or the Chorus – it seems to get squeezed as it does so.

As you may have worked out, the Phaser also works by duplicating the audio signal. The difference is that rather than delaying one copy of the audio signal significantly, it changes the phase of the wave. This is just like the Phase pot on oscillator 2 of SubSynth – it slightly alters the timing of the waveforms so that they interfere with one another. Whereas the Flanger and Chorus do so at the millisecond level, the Phaser does this at a phase level – so the actual waveforms themselves, at extremely short intervals.

A slight alteration of the phase will create a significantly different interference – which is why the Phaser also contains an LFO. This LFO has three parameters:

· Low – this is the lowest frequency that the phaser will sweep to (i.e. effect)

· High – this is the highest frequency that the phaser will sweep to (i.e. effect)

· Rate – this is the rate at which the LFO oscillates

There are two other controls on the Phaser:

· Depth – this is the degree to which the Phaser affects the signal. This is no different to Wet on the other effects this chapter has explored.

· F.Back - just like on the Flanger, the Phaser is able to feed the altered signal back into itself, amplifying the effect.

Play your sequence now, turning your Depth all the way to 5 o'clock for maximum effect. I'd suggest turning your Low to 7pm and High to 5pm respectively to hear the full range of the Phaser:

Now experiment with the Rate. Do you notice how a slow Rate seems to let your sequence breathe with a more subtle effect, but a fast Rate makes the effect take over in its own right?

Now turn F.Back all the way to the far right, around 7pm. Can you hear the whistling caused by the signal feeding back into itself?

To illustrate the difference between the Phaser and Flanger, this image is helpful:

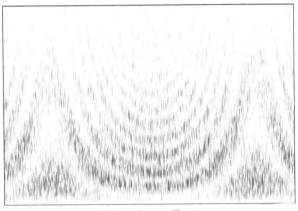

Flanging effect

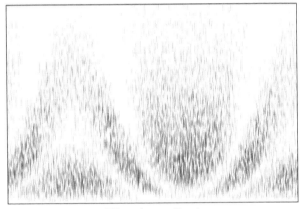

Phasing effect

This is a spectrogram of the different effects of the two modulation effects on noise. A spectrogram analyses frequency content (from top to bottom) over time (from left to right). Do you notice how the Flanging effect creates small ripples of loud and soft over the frequency range, whereas the Phasing effect creates big, sweeping changes in the frequency range? This explains why Chorus has a more subtle, sonorous sound, whereas the Phaser creates big, sweeping changes in your sound.

Exercises – Q&A

1) What's the difference between Depth and Wet/Dry?

2) What's the difference between the delay in the Chorus and the delay in a Delay unit?

3) Why does mixing the signal with itself, at a delay, create the Chorus effect?

4) Why does a long Delay setting on a Chorus make it sound like there's two distinct sounds?

5) What does F.Back on a Flanger do?

6) What's the difference between a flanger and a phaser?

7) Why are Chorus, Flanger and Phaser all in the same category, i.e. modulation effects?

If you need any help, the answers are in Appendix A.

Exercises – Practice

Experiment with different combinations of modulation effects to create an interesting, unique sound. Don't forget to remove these effects before you start the next chapter!

Chapter 16 - Parametric Equalization

In this chapter, you're going to use Parametric Equalization to alter the sound of your sequence. In order to understand Parametric Equalization, it's worth working through a little theory first.

As stated earlier, the audible frequency range is 20Hz to 20kHz. Equalization is a process that allows you to selectively boost or cut the volume of particular parts of this frequency range. Even if you've never used equalization in a music-making capacity before, it's likely you've used it somewhere, for example a Bass Boost button on a stereo. If you've worked with DJ equipment or mixers before, you'll have used equalizers like the below to adjust your sound:

Parametric Equalization is not too different to equalizers you've used in the past - the only difference is that Parametric Equalizer allows you to pick and choose which parts of the frequency range you alter.

Remove any existing effects and add a Parametric Equalizer:

The Parametric Equalizer has four functions:

· Display (at the top, it's currently a flat horizontal line). This will tell you how the equalizer is affecting your sound.

· Frequency (labeled as Freq.). This allows you to choose which frequency to alter.

· Gain. This is the extent to which the volume of the selected frequency is increased or decreased in volume.

· B.Width. This is how much of the frequency range is boosted or cut around the centre point selected by Frequency. If you're familiar with music technology, you may have previously encountered this function labeled as Q.

The display is useful in that it allows you to visualise the audible frequency range from left to right - low frequencies such as basses and rumbles on the left, and high frequencies such as tambourines, violins and triangles on the right.

You don't need to play your sequence yet - simply turn your Gain down as far left as it will go, and move your Freq pot back and forth:

You can work out visually what this will do - it will suppress frequencies towards the centre of the audible range. Play your sequence and listen to the effect.

Now try moving your Frequency pot back and forth with your sequence playing. Listen to the effect it has on your sound. You'll notice that moving it to the far-right suppresses the high end of your sequence. Moving it to the far-left suppresses the low end of your sequence, as expected. You may hear some slight flanging as you move the Frequency pot - this is an artefact of the change in frequency - it is not an effect that will continue once you stop moving the Frequency pot.

Now move your Frequency pot back into the middle, and start experimenting with the Bandwidth pot (labeled as B.Width). You'll notice that moving it to the left removes a very small slice of your frequency range, whereas moving it to the right removes a large chunk of your frequency range. An example of effective use of this function would be if you wanted to remove the bass from your sequence. Try keeping the Bandwidth at midday and moving the Frequency and Gain in order to cut the low end from your sequence. Did you notice that even at this configuration, which is clearly the most logical configuration, it didn't sound right?

This is because your sequence is mostly around middling frequencies with a small sprinkling of low-end - but to set the EQ as we have above means that only the lowest part of your sequence - a proportion so small that it's barely audible - is cut.

The solution is to turn the bandwidth up, so that now the whole low end and some of the lower middle frequencies are cut:

In a real production environment, the use of the parametric EQ is to customise the sound that your instruments make so that they gel well together. For example, the cut you've made above would be perfect for your sequence if you had a fairly prevalent bassline in your track playing in addition to your sequence, as both the lower end of your sequence and your bassline would occupy the same part of the audible spectrum, leading to both sounding dull. Making this cut would make your bassline more audible to the listener, as you've given it room to breathe.

Another use for parametric EQ is to sharpen a particular part of the frequency spectrum of a track. To highlight this, leave the current parametric EQ in place and load another below it:

Turn the Gain up on this new Parametric EQ to about 2pm:

Use the Freq and B.width controls to highlight a particular part of your sequence to the listener. This is what I came up with. For me, it highlights and brightens the top-end of the sequence and would bring that section of the sequence to the attention of the listener:

Don't forget that these two parametric equalizers are working in tandem with one another, so the curve being applied to your track is essentially a combination of the two curves. In many ways, Caustic's Parametric EQ is very basic compared to others out there. For example, Ableton's EQ Eight allows you to control up to eight sections of the EQ curve. The eight controls down the left effectively allow you to add up to 8 different equalizations across one unit – you simply select one at a time:

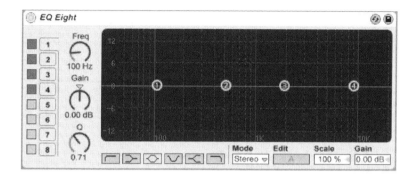

I hope this chapter has given you sufficient grounding in EQ to apply it to your own sounds. For a more in-depth discussion of EQ, I recommend *What's The Frequency* by Paul White and Matt Houghton - currently available for free on *Sound On* Sound's website via a brief internet search.

Exercises – Q&A

1) What's the difference between a 3-dial equalizer on a DJ mixer and parametric equalization?

2) What's the function of the display on a parametric equalizer?

3) What's the function of the Frequency pot?

4) What's the function of the Bandwidth pot?

5) What's the function of the Gain pot?

6) Why would you want to cut the lower end of a sequence or melody playing in the middle of a frequency range, if you also had a bassline playing?

If you need any help, the answers are in Appendix A.

Exercises – Practice

1) Use different combinations of Parametric EQ to highlight different parts of your sequence. Try creating a heavy, wooden sound and try creating the complete opposite - a light, airy sound.

Chapter 17 - Compression

Compression, also known as Dynamic Range Compression, is one of the most important effects used in recorded music. Put simply, Compression is used to even up the quieter and louder parts of an audio signal. For example, imagine you had a recording of people conversing in a room. Some people are speaking loudly, others are whispering. A compressor is the tool you would use to make both the loud conversation and the whispered conversation equally audible. It would do this by lowering the volume of the loudest parts of the conversation so that they're at a similar volume to the whispered parts – thereby allowing you to raise the volume of the whispers as loud as you can.

Compression is used in the same way in music – it quietens the loudest parts of a recording so that the overall volume can be raised without the sound distorting from being too loud. It is often used to create the final version of a track to make it as loud as possible. For example, this is a song before being compressed. Do you notice how some parts of the waveform are bigger than others, meaning they're louder than others? This difference between the loudest part and the quietest part is called dynamic range:

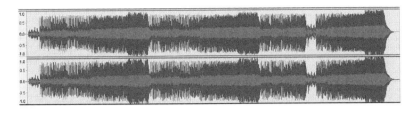

©Cody Peterson / Wikimedia Commons / CC-BY-3.0

This is the song after compression:

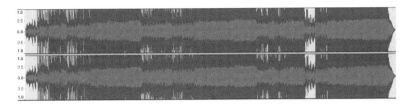

©Cody Peterson / Wikimedia Commons / CC-BY-3.0

Compare the two. Do you notice how the loudest parts of the song have stayed at a similar volume before and after compression, but the quieter parts of the song have become much louder? This is because the compression used has reduced the dynamic range.

As an aside, this compression used on finished tracks has significant repercussions for recorded music. Back in the 1940s and 1950s, before a lot of compression was applied to final tracks, jukeboxes and radio station record players were set to fixed levels. It was thought that louder tracks would stand out more to listeners, and because compressed tracks can be turned up louder, more compression was applied. Tracks became more and more compressed over subsequent decades in an arms race driven by a

115

desire for louder music – an arms race which would be dubbed the 'loudness war'. To compare, this is a track mastered in 1983:

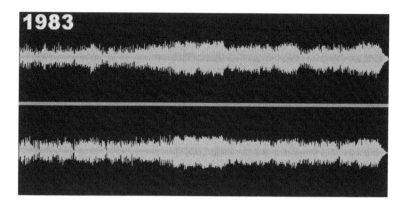

This is the same track remastered in 2000. Not only is it far louder, but the differences caused by peaks and troughs in the song's volume have been dulled:

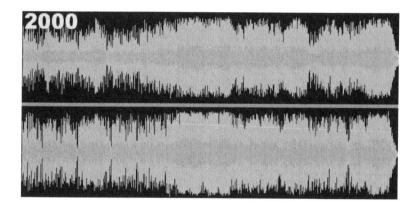

Many audio engineers believe that this compression is to the detriment of the recorded song, as the drama of quieter and louder sections is suppressed due to compression lessening the dynamic range. If you're interested, I'd certainly recommend Emmanuale

116

Deruty's article *'Dynamic Range' and the Loudness War in Sound on Sound*, freely available on the internet as of writing.

Regardless of the implications of compression, I hope this explanation has put across one of the hardest effects in music technology to understand. As well as on finished songs, compression can be used to very good effect on individual tracks, which is what we're going to do here.

In order to experience the power of compression on your sequence, turn the volume up on your SubSynth to about 3pm:

Go to your effects section, and then add a Delay in the top position. Configure it to your liking, using what you've learned in the Delay section of the Delay Effects chapter (or copy my example here if you're not sure):

Once you're happy with the sound, add a compressor below it, so that together your effects rack looks like this:

You may immediately notice a subtle difference – your sound is somehow crunchier and punchier. Let's look at the first two controls:

· Threshold tells the compressor at what threshold of volume it should start working. Anything below the Threshold level passes through unaffected, and anything above the Threshold level gets compressed. The further to the left your pot is set, the more of the signal gets compressed.

· Ratio is the extent to which the compressor reduces the volume of anything above the level set by the Threshold. It is a mathematical ratio, so when it's set to a low setting, very little compression is applied. When it's set to a high setting, a great deal of compression is applied. This handy graphic explains compression ratios well – the lower settings are towards the right of the pot, and higher settings towards the left:

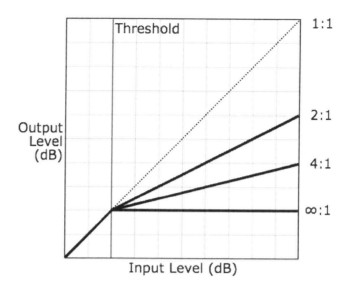

By Iain Fergusson (Own work) [Public domain], via Wikimedia Commons

For example, a 4:1 compression ratio means that every unit of volume that arrives at the compressor gets its gain reduced 4 times – or quartered. A 2:1 compression ratio means that every unit of volume that arrives at the compressor is halved in volume.

Let's experiment with these controls to understand them further. We know that the Threshold pot changes the threshold at which compression begins to apply. On this basis, turn your Threshold pot all the way to the left:

You may notice that the levels display (next to S.Chain) lights up in green. This is an indicator of the amount of gain reduction being applied to your track (in other words, the amount of volume that the compressor is removing). Now move the Threshold pot all the way to the right:

Do you notice how your track has seemingly become louder, and the gain reduction display now displays nothing? This is because little to no gain reduction is being applied to your track, because the threshold at which your compressor starts reducing gain is so high that your audio signal does not meet it.

Bring your Threshold back down to the far left to hear the compression in action again:

The next two pots, whose names you may be familiar with, are:

· Attack. This defines how long it takes for the compressor to start its gain reduction process after a signal over the threshold has been detected.
· Release. This defines how long it takes for the compressor to stop its gain reduction process after the initial gain reduction has been applied.

Now let's test these two. Turn your Attack all the way to the left:

You should notice that your signal now sounds dirty, and that the volume is pumping up and down incoherently. This is because you have the Threshold set low and the Ratio set high – so the compressor is compressing everything it detects, and doing so immediately.

Now turn your Release all the way to the far right:

You should notice that it sounds similar, except there's less pumping of the audio level. This is because the compressor is quickly compressing everything it detects, but it's applying the gain reduction for a long period before it releases the signal.

One interesting, effective use of compression here would be to emphasise the start of the note and its delays, but not the end, effectively making the start of the note louder. This is the true skill in compression – finding the 'sweet spot' to do this. Turn your Release just above far left (around 8pm), and experiment with your Attack until you find what you think sounds like the correct place. I found this configuration to be effective:

Alone, this configuration may not sound drastically different from the original, but when you're in a real production environment the extra crispness added by some effective compression can make a sequence such as this one stand out amongst the other sounds you have in a track.

Now let's explore the final function of the Compressor - and one of the most important functions. For this, you'll require a drum track. Follow these instructions to create one.

Click on the Devices menu in the bottom left:

Then, click on the + next to Device slot 2:

Select a Beatbox:

Click on Select Kit:

Select a 909. Those of you familiar with electronic music history may be aware that this will be samples of a Roland 909 drum machine:

You'll be presented with this view. Turn the volume (in the top-right corner) all the way to the right:

I'll show you how to properly program a drum synthesizer in a later chapter, but for now, scroll down to your sequence, and enter the below sequence - a basic kick drum:

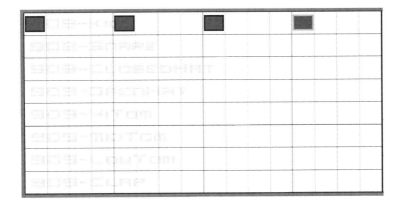

Play your sequence - you will now hear the kick drum playing in addition to your sequence.

Scroll back down to the effects:

You are about to use a function called Sidechain (called S.Chain here). The function of Sidechain is to use an external signal to trigger the compression, instead of the audio signal routed into the Compressor. Click on S.Chain so that it displays 2 (i.e. Track 2, your drums):

Now play your sequence again. Listen carefully - do you notice how your synthesizer sound is now bouncing under your kick drum?

It may not sound perfect - this is the point when you alter the Attack and Release settings to give it a better bounce. Experiment until the
128

bounce sounds good to you. This is the configuration I came up with:

To hear the sidechain effect in its full context, scroll up to your drum machine, and press M on your kick drum to mute it:

Do you hear how the bouncing effect ceases when you do this? This is because the kick drum is no longer present to trigger the compression. Click on M again to unmute the kick drum. Do you hear how it begins to bounce again?

Sidechain compression is an effect put to great use by electronic music producers - it can create a lot of tension and release as the kick drum enters and leaves the sonic stage. Here are two examples you should listen to:

1) *Not Exactly* by *Deadmau5*. Listen to the loudness and sharpness of the synthesizers used when the track starts to break at 1:30 - and how the synthesizers seem to bounce at 2:00 when the drums re-enter the stage.

2) *Many Reasons* by *Joris Voorn*. This is an example of sidechain used to great effect on a bass. It's a rolling, minimal, deep bass, but listen to how the bass grabs your attention around 2:50 when the kick ceases, as if the bassline is exhaling, and how it sounds crushed under the weight of the kick at 3:34 when the kick starts again. It's subtle, but hugely effective.

Now you understand sidechain compression, you may start to hear it a lot in electronic music production - it's used especially on basses, pads and noise sweeps. It truly is one of the most powerful effects found in the arsenal of any self-respecting electronic music producer.

In addition to the Compressor, Caustic also has a Limiter. This is a form of compression used for a specific purpose - so we'll only touch on it briefly, however the knowledge you've gleaned from learning about compression will come in handy. Remove your Compressor, and replace it with a Limiter:

Whereas a Compressor allows you to apply dynamic gain reduction according to a predefined (or external) threshold and allows you to define a ratio of gain reduction, a Limiter has a fixed threshold and will reduce the gain as much as possible to prevent the sound from breaching that threshold - on the Compression ratio diagram it effectively has an infinite threshold:

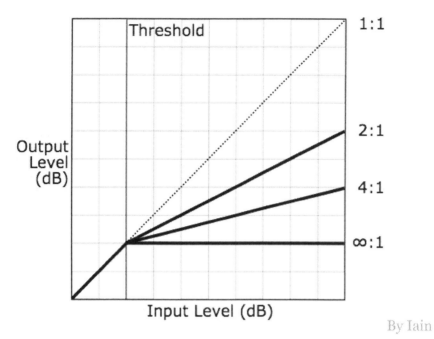

Threshold 1:1 2:1 4:1 ∞:1

Output Level (dB)

Input Level (dB)

By Iain Fergusson (Own work) [Public domain], via Wikimedia Commons

Caustic's Limiter has four features, of which Attack and Release you should already be familiar with:

· Pre - this is the extent to which the audio is amplified before it enters the Limiter

· Post - this is the extent to which the audio is amplified after it has been processed by the Limiter

· Attack. This defines how long it takes for the Limiter to start its gain reduction process after a signal has been detected.

· Release. This defines how long it takes for the Limiter to stop its gain reduction process after the initial gain reduction has been applied.

In order to hear the Limiter in action, play your sequence. As it's playing, then turn Pre as far to the right as it can go, and then bring Attack as far left as it can go. You should see the Limiter's level display light up:

By increasing Pre to its maximum volume, you're forcing the Limiter to apply itself to your track.

While your sequence plays, turn Post up as far as it can go. You may notice that your sound starts to distort. This is because despite the fact that you've applied the Limiter, you're pushing the signal into the point at which it distorts *after* the compression has occurred.

A Limiter is useful as a blunt tool, in that it can increase the volume of a single track without any of the bouncing or dynamic changes that come with using a Compressor. It's also useful for extreme compression, when your sound has a large dynamic range and you

133

want to even the volume of it. It is a vital tool when mastering a finished song (and is one of the most utilised tools in the loudness war mentioned earlier). However, for any advanced, dynamic, or interesting effects you may wish to stick with the compressor.

As an author, I do feel like I could write a whole book about compression - we have only scratched the surface here, and Caustic's compressor only scratches the surface of features available in a lot of compressors. If you would like to read a bit more about compression, I recommend *Compression Made Easy* in *Sound On Sound*'s website and *Understanding Compression* on Resident Advisor's website.

Feel free to save the progress you've made, as we're going back to pure synthesizer programming in the next chapter.

Exercises – Q&A

1) If your signal has a loud sound and a quiet sound, how does compression even the two?
2) What is dynamic range?
3) What does threshold do?
4) Why doesn't the compressor do anything if you set your threshold too high?
5) What is ratio?
6) If Ratio is set at 3:1, how loud will the output signal above the threshold be compared to the input signal?

7) What does Attack control?

8) What does Release do?

9) What is sidechain?

10) Where in electronic music are you likely to hear sidechain compression in action?

11) What's the difference between a Compressor and a Limiter?

12) What does Pre and Post do on a Limiter?

If you need any hclp, the answers are in <u>Appendix A</u>.

Exercise – Practice

Set up a sidechain with a kick drum (without referencing this chapter, if possible!) and create different effects using the sidechain. For example, try giving it a huge bounce, then try making the bouncing effect barely noticeable but whilst still applying dynamic gain. I'll give you a clue - the gain reduction display will tell you whether or not the compressor is working on your track!

Chapter 18- Creating a Bass

In this chapter, you're going to create two common bass sounds from scratch. These are:

· General bassline

· Sub-bass – this is a deeper bass, on lower notes – one that's designed more to be felt than heard.

Let's start by creating a general bassline. Load up a new Caustic file with the Init patch you created on a SubSynth.

Copy my sequence below - this is actually a bassline I used on a track that got signed a while back. Its role was to underpin the whole track with some funk, and so as a bassline it was written to draw a lot of attention to itself. If you're musically experienced then feel free to use a different one, but this sequence will give you a good start if not. Please note that I've dragged the keyboard down so that I'm working from octave C2 to C3:

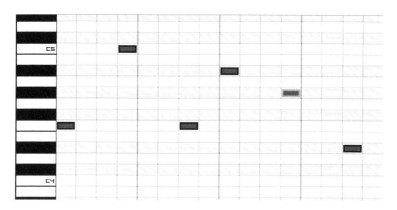

Given that the role of this bass is to draw some attention to itself, it's fair to say you need some harmonic content in the oscillators used. Whilst bass sits on the lower end of the audible threshold, thereby underpinning a song, the harmonic content of a bassline is actually hugely important. For example, listen to *Blue Monday* by *New Order*. The bass comes in around the 30 second mark. Listen to how the bass underpins the track, but it has a distinctive character to it – thereby transforming it from a sound that solely underpins a track to a sound that the whole track is built around. This is the importance of harmonic overtones in a bass. Given that you're looking for harmonic overtones in your bass, make oscillator 1 a sawtooth:

Sounds a bit much, doesn't it? Add an inverted LP filter with full Track to temper the high end of the bassline whilst emphasising the higher notes. There's no harm in adding a bit of Attack to the filter envelope to give the individual notes a bit of movement, too:

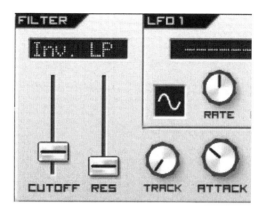

Now you should give the bass a bit of - well, bass. You'll have noticed that it currently sounds pretty hollow. A sine wave on oscillator 2 would be good for depth, but it doesn't contain enough harmonic content for a bassline that seeks to draw some attention, so go for a square wave on oscillator 2:

This step may be controversial, but I feel like this bassline requires some constructive and destructive interference. You can achieve this by moving Cents to about 11 o'clock:

Next, you may have noticed that the envelope of the sound is fairly flat. You can make it pop out a bit using the volume envelope. Turn the Sustain and Release to zero (far left), then raise the decay just past 9 o'clock. You'll require some fine adjustments here, as very small movements on the Decay can clip the sound too much or prevent it from popping to the extent you want it to:

Next, create a bit of drama over the course of the bassline using an LFO on the filter cutoff. You want the drama to happen slowly to draw the listener's attention, so assign LFO 1 to the filter cutoff, and add a slow-moving triangle LFO at the maximum possible depth:

This sounds OK, but to truly make it sound like a bassline requires some effects. Scroll down to the Effects section, then add a Parametric EQ.

It's crude, but the bottom end of this bassline needs to be louder – so that it sounds like a proper bassline! Think about how basslines in tracks you listen to seem to 'fill' the lower end, thereby underpinning the track – you want to achieve the same effect here. Therefore, the frequency you will be applying EQ to will be low and the gain will be at its maximum, as will the bandwidth:

Finally, to give the bassline a bit of character, add a Reverb. Turn the Wet of your Reverb up to full to hear the effect it's having.

The first setting to alter is Room, because currently the room sounds far too big! Bring it down to about 8pm.

Next up is Damp. You don't want the Reverb muddying the lower end of your track too much, so turn Damp up all the way to 5 o'clock.

Then, it's time to modify the Delay. You want the Delay that you add to the reverb to sound subtle and organic, so you can bring the Delay right down to 9 o'clock.

Up next is the width - this is a subjective topic, but in music production it's bad practice to have any stereo width on the lower end, so bring the width right down to its furthest left setting, around 7 o'clock.

Finally, and most important, is the Wet setting. Experiment with this value until you find the point at which the Reverb is having an effect, but the effect remains subtle. I decided on about 10 o'clock:

Congratulations - you've just programmed a bass from scratch! Feel free to save your patch using SubSynth's in-built menu, because it's now time to create a new Caustic file with a fresh Init Caustic patch to create a sub-bass.

A sub-bass couldn't be any more different in its role than a general bassline. A sub-bass is designed to underpin the whole track without drawing too much attention to itself. In a club setting, it's designed to be felt, rather than heard. To quote the veteran Bass producer Pinch, *"If your chest ain't rattling, it ain't happening"*. It's at a lower frequency range than a normal bass.

Some great examples of sub-bass include Mala's *Lean Forward*, Kahn's *Way Mi Defend* and High Contrast's *If We Ever*.

The key aspect of sub-bass is that it's deep, low and very bassy. Its depth comes from the fact that the oscillators used don't create a lot of harmonic content and can therefore concentrate on pushing out the energy required to create a deep bass.

On that basis, create a simple sequence to reflect this role. I suggest you copy mine below, paying attention to the fact that the keyboard is set to octave C1-C2, and therefore dragging the piano roll down if necessary:

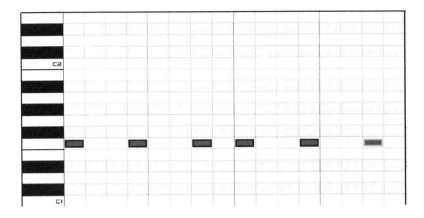

Our starting point is a sine wave, as you don't need harmonic content – you need sheer power:

Play your sequence. If you can't hear anything but the meter next to the Volume pot is green, you may need better speakers! Try a good pair of studio monitors or headphones.

Assuming you can hear it, it sounds pretty good already, doesn't it? I've successfully created and used sub-basses in tracks that consist of a single sine wave. However, it's useful to have a small amount of harmonic content in the sound, even if it's barely heard - this will add warmth and depth to the sub-bass. Change oscillators 1 and 2 to Triangle waves:

If you play the sequence now, you will notice that harmonic content is coming through, but it sounds ugly. The best solution for this is a LP filter to crush these higher harmonics, but leave a few lurking at the bottom end of your sound:

Next, add a small amount of Release to make the notes sound more natural, but without colliding with one another:

Now the fundamentals are in place, it's time for some effects to strengthen the sound.

Firstly, just like the general bass, some parametric EQ will be useful in boosting the lowest frequencies. Because of the oscillators used, this patch is already much bassier than the general bass you worked on earlier in this chapter, so less gain and bandwidth range is required when boosting the low end:

Now to add a bit of warmth and volume, you should use a Limiter, due to its ability to boost volume. Some slow attack with slow release will allow the bass to breathe, and a small amount of Pre gain will enhance the amount of compression added. A small

145

amount of Post gain will be useful to bring the sub-bass to the correct degree of volume:

And there we have it! A sub-bass that's full of character and warmth.

The good news is that most basses you'll come across in electronic music will contain characteristics used in both the sub-bass and the general bass. On that basis, I'll leave it up to you to experiment.

Exercises – Q&A

1) Why would you add an LP filter to a bass?
2) What are the steps taken to provide character within this bassline, before adding effects? There are five.
3) Why is it important to increase the volume of the lower frequencies using a Parametric EQ?
4) How is a sub-bass different to a bass?

If you need any help, the answers are in <u>Appendix A</u>.

Exercises – Practice

1) Create three different bass patches based on your favourite pieces of electronic music. These patches don't have to sound identical to your favoured sound, but they should be a decent approximation.

Chapter 19 - Creating a Pad

In this chapter, you will create a basic pad. If you've not heard of a pad before, you will probably still know what one is without knowing the name for it! A pad performs a role in electronic music similar to strings in contemporary music - it adds mood or depth, but doesn't tend to draw *too* much attention (although this is a rule that can be intentionally violated).

For examples of pads, listen to the following:

Surplus by *Skudge* - the pad is the very long chord note that you can hear at the very start of the track, but slowly increases in volume until it's the primary focus of the track around 5 minutes in.

Sky Hunt by *DJ Steaw* - the pad starts to increase in volume until it draws your full attention around 1:19. Bonus points if you spot the modulation effects on the pad!

Screaming Hands (Tuff City Kids Dreamscape UK Mix) by *Radioslave* - the pad begins at the start of the track and carries it in its entirety.

As you have heard, pads are lush, rich in harmonic content and slow-moving. In order to program one, let's start with the sequence. Because it's a long, slow sound, let's create a long, slow sequence.

Firstly, create a new SubSynth and load your Init patch. Then, scroll down to your sequence. Rather than program it in as usual, click on the Grid button (next to Size):

Then click on 2x to make your sequence 2 bars long:

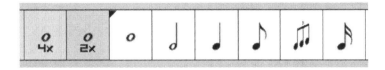

Click *Yes* when it asks you if you want to grow your pattern to 2 measures:

Now you've expanded your available pattern to 2 bars, it's time to enter some musical notes. Again, if you're musically experienced, feel free to enter your own slow, winding chords, but if not I suggest using mine:

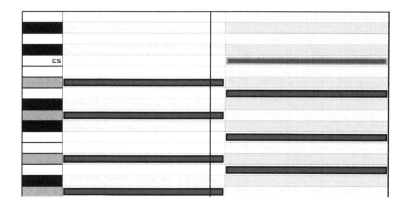

Now play your sequence. With it playing, scroll up to SubSynth.

If you think about the properties of a pad - long, slow notes and harmonically rich content, some programming ideas may come to mind.

Given that you're looking for harmonically rich content, select a sawtooth on each of your oscillators:

Harsh, isn't it?

Create some harmonic interference by moving the Cents on
oscillator 2 to 1pm:

As you can hear, a filter is now required in order to filter out those
harsh unwanted frequencies. You may have noticed that pads seem
to float in the middle-high part of the hearing register, so make it a
Band-Pass filter with some resonance to give it that added bit of
harmonic bite – this is because, as discussed in the chapter about
filters, Band-Pass filters allow frequencies through around a centre
point – in this case the middle of the audible spectrum:

Please note, of course, that Low Pass and High Pass filters also have
their uses when programming Pads – however I tend to find Band
Pass to be the most effective filter type.

You may have also noticed that something about a pad seems inherently slow - this is all in the envelopes.

The first thing to look at is the volume envelope - you want the sound to rise slowly and hang on for a bit after the key has been released.

On that basis, set your attack a bit slower (around 10 o'clock) and set your Release a bit longer, so that the note continues to linger after the key is released:

Next, you want this sort of movement to also be reflected in the filter - so turn the Attack up on your filter envelope as high as it will go - this is so that in the time it takes for the Attack of your envelope to reach its maximum, you've already changed note. So in essence, with every new note your filter rises:

Finally, some additional interference can be created by altering the phase of oscillator 2. However, it seems rather dull to do so statically, as this will create a single effect that doesn't change – and the character of pads are all about slow, lush evolution. You're better off using LFO 1 to dynamically and slowly alter the phase of oscillator 2 in relation to oscillator 1:

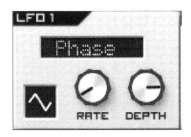

What you can hear now is both the Cents pot and the LFO-altered phase working together to create a lot of beautiful harmonic interference.

Next, let's look at effects.

You would be very reasonable to believe that a modulation effect would be useful here - and keep that in mind for the exercises at the end of this chapter, but in this instance I want the beauty of this sound to reflect back upon itself to create even more pleasant harmonic interference – so that there are copies of the evolution of this sound in different states echoing around. On this basis, I suggest you add a Delay.

A slow delay is best for this, with a fair amount of stereo feedback - I find this gives the pad an ethereal sense:

Then, the effect can be enhanced by adding a Reverb. With this sort of sound, there's no need to be subtle, so you can pick a large room with no dampness, and add a fair amount of width and delay to the reverb signal:

There we have it! You've gone from creating a deep, booming bass to creating a floating pad - using precisely the same synthesizer. This is the beauty of synthesis - the versatility of sounds at your fingertips.

In the next chapter, we're going to look at creating a lead, but not before you do the following exercises:

Exercises – Q&A

1) Why wouldn't a fast sequence of notes work when programming a pad?

2) Why would you want to use a Band Pass filter for a pad?

3) Why is the Attack on the Filter Envelope turned higher up than the Attack on the Volume Envelope in the patch I showed you?

4) Why did I choose to alter the phase of oscillator 2 using an LFO instead of changing it on LFO2's settings?

5) Why does a Delay and Reverb work so well?

If you need any help, the answers are in <u>Appendix A</u>.

Exercises - Practice

1) Return to your SubSynth patch, and try various combinations of filters and filter envelopes. While you do this, think about the variation in sound you can glean, and where each sound might fit in a piece of music.

2) Return to your effects combinations and try different modulation effects, making a note of the impact they have on your pad sound.

Chapter 20 - Creating a Lead

In this chapter, you'll learn what a lead is and, most importantly, how to create one.

Firstly, what is a lead synth? As you can gather from the name, a lead 'leads' the track. It is usually a monophonic (i.e. a single note) melody that runs across the middle to upper frequency range of a track. It plays a similar role to a guitar solo in a piece of music.

Examples of leads include:

· The squeaky synth melody during the introduction of *(Not Just) Knee Deep* by *Funkadelic*

· The synth melody in *Das Model* by *Kraftwerk*

· The whistling melody heard in the background of *Let Me Ride* by *Dr Dre*

If you're still struggling to pick out a lead synth, search on the internet for videos titled 'Lead Synth' - you'll soon get the idea.

Now you're going to program one on SubSynth. This will be fairly simple, but due to the melodic nature of the lead, you're going to use an advanced feature of Caustic - this is because you're going to play the keys, to give it that free, improvisational feel.

Load a SubSynth and an Init patch for it, then click the - button above Polyphony to make your Polyphony setting 1. This is because as a monophonic lead, you're only ever going to want to play one note at a time. Even if you play two notes at the same time by accident, keeping your Polyphony setting at 1 will mean that only one note will play – this allows you, as a keyboard player, to play with much more freedom:

Then, click on the three bars at the bottom-left of Caustic:

Then, click on Scale at the far bottom right:

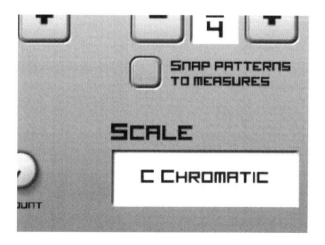

In essence, a Scale is a set of notes ordered by pitch. You can use the Scale feature to pick out notes that will sound good together if you play them using your touchscreen or mouse.

A natural scale for a synth lead is Blues Minor. The reason for this is beyond the scope of this book, but if you're interested then *Composition for Computer Musicians* by *Michael Hewitt* is an excellent guide.

Select Blues Minor and click on Done in the bottom right:

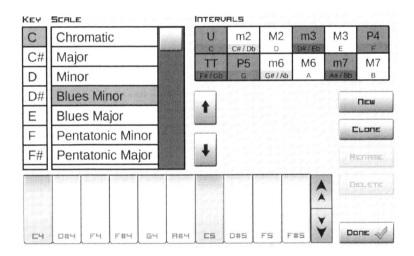

Now you're ready! Play some keys on the on-screen keyboard.

You'll notice it already sounds pretty good. Give it a bit of character using a sawtooth oscillator:

Play your notes again. Have you noticed that this sounds so good, you could realistically call this a lead in its own right? That's the simplicity of a good monophonic lead. However, there's certainly additional ways we can add funk to the sound.

Firstly, it currently sounds a little bit harsh. Add a LowPass filter, but only filter the sound slightly. Then, turn Track up to about 9 o'clock so that the higher notes shine more brightly:

Now you can make the sound a bit funkier by adding some intentional vibrato, thereby slightly detuning and retuning the sound.

Go to LFO 1, and make the LFO 1 destination Osc 1+2. This will drive the LFO to alter the frequency of your oscillators. Turn the rate up high (around 2pm), and add a small amount of depth:

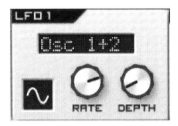

Play some notes now. Do you notice how funky it sounds now? A static note seems to move around in place.

Some additional movement can be added by sending a similar, slower LFO to the filters. Send LFO 2 to the filter cutoff, with your Rate around midday and a small amount of depth - think of it as seasoning for the sound:

Now the sound is ready for effects. If you're staying true to the lead, there's only one effect I'd suggest - parametric EQ. By cutting the low end of your lead using the parametric EQ, you can allow the lead to sit gently on top of the other instrumentation in your track. Don't forget that you used parametric EQ to increase the bass on a bassline in an earlier chapter – removing the bass from your lead would give the imaginary bassline much more room to breathe:

Reasonably speaking, that's it for this chapter - you've created a lead! However, there's a couple of other ideas that we can look at.

If you're looking for a drier, more mellow lead, I'd suggest changing oscillator 1 to a square wave, and removing all depth from your LFOs:

Now play some notes. Do you notice the massive change in emotion and context caused by the simple oscillator change? That's what synthesis is all about!

You could even make it more mellow by changing oscillator 1 to a sine wave:

Or, to make the brashest, loudest lead possible, change oscillator 1 back to a sawtooth:

Then, add another oscillator, and turn the Cents up 7 steps. That way, you're creating a harmonic fifth (i.e. you're playing notes C and G at the same time), and it's as if, in spite of the monophonic mode, you're playing two notes at the same time. In addition, you can add some harmonic interference by turning the Cents pot slightly:

Turn your LFOs back up slightly:

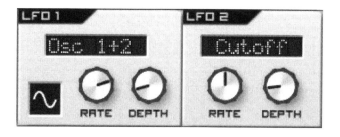

There we have it! A brash, aggressive lead.

This concludes the chapter on leads, where you've explored the spectrum of leads, from mellow to harsh. Creating them really is that simple!

Exercises – Q&A

1) Why would you want to set the Polyphony setting to 1?

2) How does selecting a different scale help you play a lead?

3) What were the steps you took to create a good-sounding lead, before you even added effects and filter?

4) What oscillator would you use for a brash lead?

5) What oscillator would you use for a mellow lead?

If you need any help, the answers are in Appendix A.

Exercises – Practice

1) Experiment creatively with leads, changing oscillator settings using the knowledge you've accumulated so far. Note or save any settings that you particularly love.

2) Add and remove the Delay and Modulation effects that you've learned about in their respective chapters, analysing the emotional statement each different sound creates.

Chapter 21 - Creating Chords

In this chapter, you're going to create some moving, dynamic chords. Whereas leads tend to be on one note, chords are a group of notes (typically three or more) played at once to create a harmony – just like someone playing chords on a guitar. These can be found in the middle frequency range of many a track. Chords are a key component of many different styles of electronic music, including Techno, House and Trance, and in my opinion, in many ways, are directly descended from the off-beat chords used in Reggae. For examples, listen to:

· *Stella* by *Jam and Spoon*. The chords are the rhythmic, pulsing sound that enter around 0:15.

· *M4.5* by *Maurizio*. A couple of layers of chords remain constant throughout this track.

· *Tense (DBridge Remix)* by *Scuba*. The chords start immediately at the introduction of the track.

Notice how the chords remain fairly constant melodically and rhythmically, and that the changes in the character of the sound itself over time creates the narrative within the tracks.

First, start by sequencing some chords. Load your SubSynth on an Init patch and scroll down to program the following notes in. If you're musically experienced, you'll recognize these as minor chords:

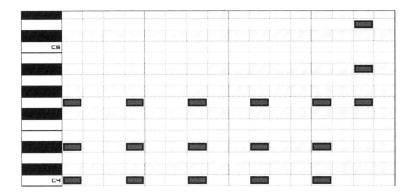

Play your sequence - if it sounds off, somehow, then make sure you've followed the sequence above to the note!

The first step is to provide a harmonically rich oscillator as a starting point. This is because a lot of the drama in chord-based tracks comes from their evolution over time, and a harmonically rich sound gives you something more interesting to evolve than a bland sound. You should know by now that I'm going to pick a sawtooth for this job!

Play your sequence. Did you notice how the tracks you listened to at the start of the chapter possessed that short, sharp character as if played on a piano? That's due to the filter and corresponding filter envelope. Firstly, set your filter to Inv. LP. This is so that the filter envelope acts in reverse upon the filter. Then, bring the cutoff down to about halfway so that the filter acts upon the sound, with res about a third of the way up for that added resonant bite:

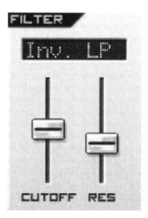

Next, turn up the Track and Attack on the filter envelope to about 10 o'clock and listen to the results by playing your sequence:

Next, it's time to automate the movement of the filter to create some dynamism. You could move the Filter cutoff yourself, but adding this LFO means that the filter will move *in addition* to your movements. Send LFO1 to the filter cutoff, with the depth around 1 o'clock and the rate as slow as possible:

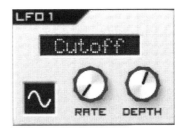

Now it's time to add another oscillator for some added depth. Set oscillator 2 to sawtooth:

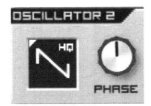

To create that bit of depth required, turn oscillator 2 down an octave - this effectively means that oscillator 2 will be playing its sequence as if C3 was the bottom note, not C4 – so you now have two chords playing at two different octaves, like you have six notes playing instead of three:

However, in spite of the chords playing different octaves, you can still create some interference by slightly moving Cents - in my case I moved it to about 12:30:

Do you notice how, now you've lowered the octave of oscillator 2, that the sound now has a great deal more weight and gravity? However, the higher oscillator rather overpowers the lower one, making the overall sound rather tinny. To alter this, move Mix in oscillator 1 to roughly three o'clock - meaning that about three quarters of the sound is comprised of oscillator 2:

Play your sequence back and listen. Do you hear how as the filter cycles, the upper oscillator (oscillator 1) just adds that bit of shine?

Now it's time to add some effects!

You may have gathered, from listening to the example tracks at the beginning of this chapter, that Delay is used routinely on tracks based around these chords. Scroll down to your effects and add a Delay:

I've set a fairly fast delay but with a long feedback time. The fast delay time is to create delays that work faster than the time between each chord, and the long feedback time is so that as the LFO brings the filter cutoff up and down, the delays continue to reflect earlier cutoff values - in effect creating an auditory collision between notes with a higher cutoff and those with a lower cutoff:

Now it's starting to sound good - but it lacks in a bit of atmosphere. This is where Reverb comes in!

Add a Reverb below the Delay - this means that the Reverb acts on not only the synthesizer itself, but also the Delay's output:

Now, there's a lot of room for subjectivity and context here, but I preferred a large room, no damping whatsoever, a short delay (so that the Reverb clings to the chords and delay, a lot of stereo width and a fairly wet sound:

My method (which I suggest you adopt) for finding the correct reverb is to turn Wet all the way to the right where it has the maximum effect on the sound. This allows you to fully hear each effect of each pot turn on the Reverb. I leave the Wet until last, as that merely adjusts the mix of the Reverb's output with its input, not the effect of the Reverb itself.

Play your sequence. That's it! In this chapter, you've created some beautiful, undulating delayed chords. Don't close the file yet, as you can use it for the exercises:

Exercises – Q&A

1) What are chords?

2) Why would you send an LFO to the filter?

3) Why would you move Oscillator 2 down an octave?

4) Why would you turn the Reverb to fully Wet when altering its settings?

If you need any help, the answers are in Appendix A.

Exercises - Practice

1) With the sequence playing, creatively create drama and tension by slowly altering the parameters of Subsynth. Make a mental note of how your changes alter the character of the sound. For example, try creating a build by increasing the Volume Envelope Release on SubSynth, then snapping it back to its lowest setting to diffuse the tension.

2) Experiment with every parameter you can, but you should especially consider these parameters:

· Volume envelope Release

· Volume envelope Attack

· Filter

· Delay Feedback

· Reverb Room size

· Reverb Wet/Dry

Chapter 22 – Recreating Sounds

In this chapter, you'll begin to synthesize (get it?) all of the knowledge that you have acquired through this book. Rather than rely on my instruction, I will ask you to rely on what you've learned so far by asking you to listen to sounds and program them into an Init patch on SubSynth. I suggest for this that you open a new Caustic document with an Init patch on your SubSynth.

The first sound I'd like you to recreate is the synthesizer sequence in *Drifting Away* by *Faithless* – the one that can be found at 0:51. If you truly want a challenge, try to program the melody into your sequencer. However if you don't wish to do that, you can glean a similar sound by programming the following melody – it's not an exact match (for copyright reasons), but it will get you in the ballpark:

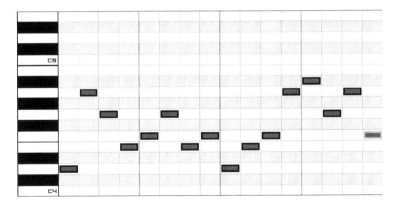

I'd suggest halving the tempo of your sequence by clicking the three lines at the bottom of your sequencer:

And setting your tempo to 60bpm:

Then, click on the arrow next to Help to return to your sequence:

Firstly, think about the properties of the sound you hear and relate it back to the oscillator summary at the beginning of the chapter on single oscillators. I've copied it below for reference:

· The sine wave is the simplest waveform, containing no harmonics. It sounds smooth and gentle.

176

· The square wave is a fairly harsh, wooden sound, containing odd harmonics.

· The triangle wave has similar bass abilities to the sine, but with a limited degree of odd harmonics in addition.

· The sawtooth is a brash, harsh sound, with a lot of harmonics.

If you listen to the sound in the Faithless track, does it seem to relate to any of these particularly well? To test your answer, go up to your SubSynth, and cycle through the oscillators until you find the one that sounds most like the sequence you've just heard in the Faithless track. Did you find it?

That's right – it's a sine wave:

However, it does not quite sound right yet. Firstly, can you hear that very subtle click happening on each note? That's to do with your volume envelope. Because the volume envelope is sensitive, that little click you hear is the Release closing down the sound instantly – so instantaneously that it creates an audible click due to the speed at which the waveform ceases to play. This means you need to turn the Release up, but not enough that the notes take so long to release that they interfere with one another:

Now play the melody again. Notice how it's lacking something when compared to Faithless' rendition? Listen to the Faithless track and try to work out which effect they're using. There's a spoiler below if you're struggling.

It's a Reverb!

Scroll down and add a Reverb, tweaking the settings until you find what sounds right to you. I'm not going to show you how to get the Reverb right, because I trust you to have worked with the Reverb enough by now to have a decent understanding. In addition, it's all a matter of opinion at this point!

Once you have the Reverb right, congratulations – you've just recreated a patch from scratch!

Let's try another track. Listen to *Greece 2000* by *Three Drives*. You're looking to recreate the trance lead that comes in around 2:30 on the 8-minute version, or around 37 seconds in on the shorter radio mix. Load up a new Caustic file and your Init patch on SubSynth, and I'll provide you some notes to start off:

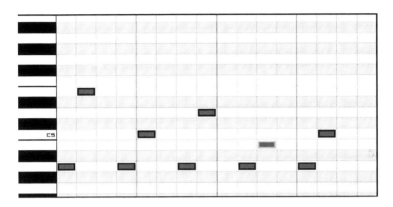

Now, listen to your notes (with the default sine wave oscillator), and then listen to the *Three Drives* track. Referring to the notes on the different oscillator types, which type of waveform do you think you're listening to? I'll clue you in, it's a harsh tone – a harmonically rich one.

Did you get it? It's a sawtooth. Select a sawtooth in Osc 1:

Play your sequence back. How does it differ from the *Three Drives* track's riff? Think about it in terms of envelopes and filtering. Try to modify your filter and envelopes, given what you know. I'll give you a clue – you require an Inv. LP filter.

If you're struggling, let me give you my thought process.

The first thing to note is that the sound seems to peak quite harshly, but disappear quickly. This indicates to me that there's very little Release or Sustain on the Volume envelope, because Sustain would make the Decay seemingly lengthen slightly and a high Release setting would mean you could hear the note after it's been played. We can also surmise from how quickly the note begins (i.e. very quickly – each note doesn't seem to fade in) that the Attack is as low as it can possibly be. Therefore we know that the key to getting the Volume envelope right is the Decay. Tweak the Decay until it sounds like we're getting closer to the original sound. I went for this:

Now that the volume envelope sounds right, have another listen to the Three Drives track and compare it to your patch. Do you notice how the top end of the track doesn't seem as harsh or as bright as your patch? We can therefore surmise there's a low-pass filter in play. However, there's a particular character to the sound – one where the sound is very bright at the start of a note but seems to lose its brightness before the note has elapsed – in a similar way to a piano note. Knowing this, we can deduce that there's a filter envelope in place, with a setting on the Attack.

Play your sequence. While playing the sequence, move your Filter Envelope Attack to 7 o'clock (you'll hear very little), and slowly move it to the right until you find what sounds like the correct point. You're getting there, aren't you? Your patch is still too bright, though. It clearly needs some filtering. Bring your cutoff down to what sounds like the correct point.

To summarise so far, your patch should look something like this:

If you play it back, it still doesn't sound quite right. Listen back to the *Three Drives* track and try to work out what it is. I'll give you a clue – it's hidden *around* the notes.

If you can hear a Delay, you're absolutely right. Add a Delay to your Insert effects and tweak your settings:

And there we have it! There's still a slight difference, but I promise you it would be imperceptible in the context of the full track's mix.

For the next one, try something a bit different – a wobble sub-bass. Listen to *Anti-War Dub* by *Mala*, listening out for the bass at the start. Not the mid - but the deep, deep sub-bass that underpins everything. If you can't hear anything, try using a good pair of headphones, or a pair of speakers with a big subwoofer. This track is a classic on huge soundsystems for a good reason!

For this, I'd suggest using Caustic's keyboard, but using the Down arrow to the right of the keyboard to bring the octave down to C1, so that you can play those lower notes:

Look back at the waveform list and think about how you'd construct that kind of sub-bass sound. It absolutely needs the smoothness and bass weight of a sine wave to start in Oscillator 1, but your second oscillator is a difficult choice. A square wave could work with sufficient filtering, but I've gone for a triangle wave. You want to add a small amount of harmonics, but not too much:

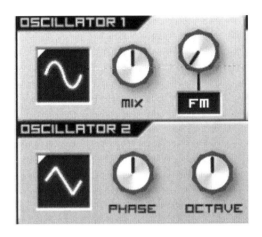

Have a play of your notes. Nice, dark and bassy, aren't they? You'll notice they, however, are lacking in wobble. What function would be able to automate a pattern, like a wobble in a synthesizer?

You're absolutely correct if you've started reaching for the LFO.

Often, with this sort of wobble, I'd suggest you add an LP filter and automate the cutoff to create that wobble. If that's what you've tried, your logic is correct – and it's definitely worth adding an LP filter with the cutoff at the bottom. However in this instance, the frequencies being played are so low, and so lacking in harmonic content (remember, you're mixing a sine wave with a triangle wave), that an LFO firing at a cutoff that's having very little effect on the sound will not suffice –your sub-bass is simply too deep!

On that basis, I'd suggest sending your LFO to your volume:

Play some notes – you've now created a dark, wobbly sub-bass!

We'll put together one more sound - a garage bassline. Listen to *Poundcake* by *Moony* – specifically the bassline that interplays with the organ around 1:27 onwards.

If I were you, I'd go back to an Init patch, but keep the octave down towards C1.

The tone used in this bassline is one that contains some bass weight, but also some harmonics, unlike the sub-bass. However, sound isn't as harsh as a sawtooth. On that basis, you should choose a square wave:

This patch is actually exceedingly simple – it just moves round a lot. Listen to how the bass evolves, squelching around, and think about which part of the synthesizer you'll need to modulate to reflect that.

If you guessed that you required a low-pass filter, you're correct. A lot of the tension in this patch also comes from the fact that the Resonance is turned significantly up.

I've picked this bassline and track because there's a lot of modulation and variation – I'm leaving it up to you to have fun with the filter, LFO and filter envelopes to try to reflect as many aspects of the bassline in *Poundcake* as you can – you've learned enough that a great step is to experiment entirely independently.

In this chapter, you have put all of the knowledge you have gleaned so far together. I hope you feel that your understanding of synthesis is more structured and rigorous by now. Our next place in the journey is to learn about drum synthesis.

Exercises – Q&A

1) Why does Release on the volume envelope create an audible click if set to its lowest setting?

2) Why didn't I think that the sound in Three Drives' track had much Release or Delay on it, considering it seemed to peak quite harshly but disappear quickly?

3) Why does the fact that the notes in Three Drives' riff don't seem to fade in at all indicate the use of a low Attack setting?

4) How can you deduce that there's a Filter Envelope in place in Three Drives' Riff?

5) Why, when creating a deep sub-bass, would you look to automate the Volume to create wobble rather than a low-pass filter?
6) Why is a Square wave used in the bassline in Moony's Poundcake?

If you need any help, the answers are in <u>Appendix A</u>.

Exercises - Practice

1) Find three more electronic music tracks that you love. Try to recreate the synthesizer sounds you hear, even if it's just a crude imitation. What's more important than a perfect recreation is to work systematically, analyzing the sound you hear and comparing it to the fundamental sounds (i.e. the oscillators) of your synthesizer. It's a fantastic feeling when you get it right!

Chapter 23 – Drum synthesis

In this chapter, we shall explore drum synthesis. This is a slight deviation from the topics we have delved into so far, as it doesn't deal explicitly with the subtractive synthesis you've learned in previous chapters. However, the ability to program drum machines is an important weapon in any producer's arsenal, and the concepts behind drum synthesis are not that far from the concepts you've been learning already within this book – so there's certainly no harm in learning drum synthesis!

Start a new document on Caustic, and instead of loading a SubSynth, load a Beatbox:

Then, click on Select Kit:

and load a 909:

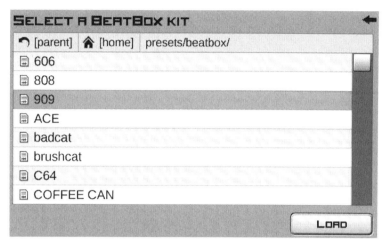

The reason you're loading a patch rather than programming one from scratch is that this type of drum machine works by loading samples (i.e. pre-made recordings). It doesn't generate any sound in of itself.

Once the kit has loaded, it's time to program some drums. As complex as it is, I recommend you take the time to input my sequence:

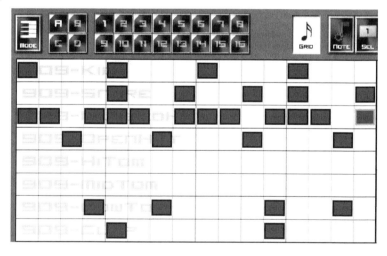

Once you've programmed the sequence, play it, and scroll up to the Beatbox. You'll see five pots next to each of the ten drums:

Tune defines the frequency at which the sample plays. Turn Tune to the right on the Kick. You'll notice that not only does the sound play at a high frequency, it plays in less time. This is because you've changed the speed at which the sample plays. Because it plays through faster, it doesn't last as long.

Punch and Decay operate in tandem. These are Attack and Decay envelopes, just like on a synthesizer. Being samples of a fixed length, it wouldn't be possible to control Sustain and Release, as the sample plays through once with each key press – holding down the key would have no effect. On that basis, think of Punch and Decay as Attack and Decay on a volume envelope:

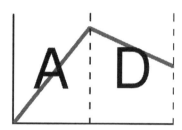

Experiment with Punch and Decay to hear the results. You'll hear Punch acting much like the Attack part of the Volume Envelope, defining how quickly the sample fades in. You'll hear Decay acting much like the Decay function on a volume envelope, controlling how long it takes the sample to return to zero volume.

Pan controls the mix of the sample between the left and right speaker. If you're using stereo speakers or headphones, experiment with the Pan pot to hear this in action.
Vol simply controls the volume of the sample.

Now you know what each pot does, you can use this to great effect to improve the loop you can hear. Working from right to left, follow my instructions.

Firstly, the clap is not loud or prominent enough for such a rhythmically important element. Turn the Vol up to about 1 o'clock and the Pan to about 11 o'clock:

You should hear that the clap is now more prominent.

The next active channel to the left is Low Tom. You can hear the sound it's making, and I believe that it draws too much attention when it should actually be underpinning the rhythm. In order to make it underpin the rhythm, bring Tune down to about 7 o'clock and Volume down to about 11 o'clock:

Next, it sounds to me like the open hi-hat is too dominant and isn't tuneful enough.

On that basis, bring the Tune down slightly, to about 11:30, bring the Decay down to 1 o'clock, Pan it slightly to the right (around 1 o'clock), as this will offset the clap that is panned slightly to the left, and turn the Volume slightly up:

Now it's the closed Hi-hat's turn. It sounds far too dominant in my opinion, and can be brought into line by turning the Decay down to about 9pm:

192

Now that's done, the snare sounds fine – so the final step is to turn the Kick up as high as possible, as that's what underpins the whole track:

Next, you're going to use a SubSynth to explore an older, more archaic method of drum synthesis – used extensively in Kraftwerk's work but still heard sporadically in modern tracks – noise shaping. Save the file you've been working on, and stop your sequence if you don't want to hear it repeating.

Click into the bottom left to add a new device, and add a SubSynth to Slot 2:

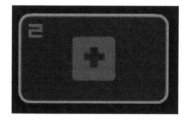

Input this pattern:

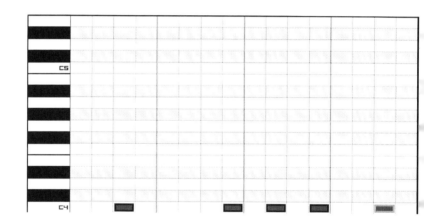

Now scroll up to your SubSynth, and change oscillator 1 to Noise:

Play your sequence. As you can hear, it sounds very brash. This is where the *shaping* aspect of noise shaping comes in – noise shaping is the science of turning that flat-sounding white noise into something with character – in this case a percussive character.

Firstly, make your filter an Inv. HP, and turn your Attack up slightly. You should hear it begin to act on your noise:

You want to shape the noise so that it's short and punchy using the

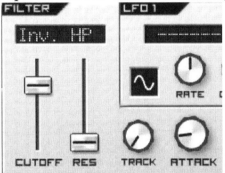

volume envelope. Turn the sustain pot left to as low as it will go, and bring Release down to about 10 o'clock, and find a sweet spot for Decay around 8 o'clock:

Next, give your noise some movement by adding a slow LFO to

modulate the cutoff:

Finally, head down to the Effects section and add a Delay to make the sound bounce around rhythmically:

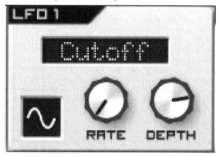

That's it! You should now hear the white noise adding a bouncy, subtle rhythm to your drum track.

In this chapter, you've created two drum tracks – one using samples, and another using sounds that you've shaped themselves. These are by far the most prevalent techniques you'll find in electronic music production, and this chapter has given you a solid grounding in both.

Exercises – Q&A

1) What does the Tune pot control?

2) What does the Punch pot control?

3) What does the Decay pot control?

4) What does the Pan pot control?

5) What does the Volume pot control?

6) What is noise shaping?

7) Why do the envelopes play such an important role in noise shaping?

If you need any help, the answers are in <u>Appendix A</u>.

Exercises - Practice

1) Find a video of Jeff Mills programming a 909 live to understand a truly impressive drum machine programming feat – searching for *Jeff Mills 909* will suffice.

2) Find an online drum machine and program it – as of writing, HTML5 Drum Machine is a good option, but online drum machines are always coming and going – search for 'free online drum machine' and you will find something!

Chapter 24 – Routing matrices

In this chapter, we're going to look at audio signal routing. Being electronic devices (or virtual simulations of electronic devices), synthesizers sometimes give us options as to how we wish to route the signals that go through them. Some hardware synthesizers allow the user to route the sound to different sections of the synthesizer using wires, as illustrated in the picture below:

Caustic, amongst other virtual synthesizers, also allows you to do this – albeit virtually.

To demonstrate this, go to Caustic, and click this button in the bottom left:

Click to add a new device:

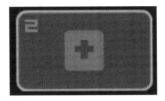

Select a Modular:

You'll be presented with this blank device:

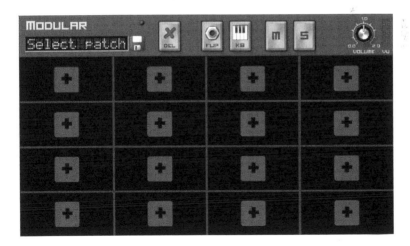

This is an entirely blank canvas! You will now be presented with the option to add different synthesizer components, effectively creating your own synthesizer from scratch!

To easily understand whether or not what you do is working, add a basic sequence below the synthesizer, and press Play so that it's constantly looping. Don't worry about the fact that you can't hear anything:

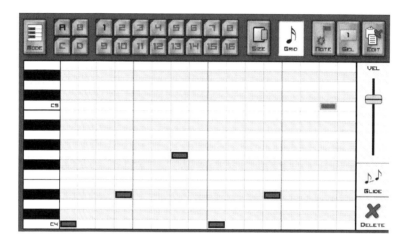

Go back to the modular synthesizer, and click on the +:

Can you guess what component you need to generate sound? Don't forget the two-step process inherent in all synthesis – the generation of sound, followed by the manipulation of the generated sound.

Hopefully you were correct – it's an oscillator, listed here as a Waveform Generator. Load it from the list:

If your sequence is playing, you may notice the little white light above the Save button flashing, indicating that it's receiving a note input. But you can't hear anything!

To hear the notes being generated, click on Flip on the top bar:

You'll be presented with this view:

It's absolutely right that you can't hear anything - because nothing is connected! When you Flip it, this is where you can connect the virtual wires. There are two types of wires – and knowing what they are, to some extent, is a matter of guesswork and logic. The two types are:

1) Audio wires. These carry audio signals, for example from one area of the synthesizer to another.

2) Data wires (known as Control Voltage, or abbreviated as CV). These carry signals that alter parameters, for example an LFO signal or an envelope signal.

Here's the structure of what you're looking at:

Effectively, the sequencer outputs on the top left are data as to what notes are being played (i.e. the notes you've programmed). Your oscillator converts this note data into audible tones, and outputs it to the Audio Output. Using your finger or mouse to drag, drag a cable from Note CV in your sequencer output to the Note input on the oscillator. This, for example, is a Data cable. Then, drag a cable from Out on the oscillator to your Audio Output. This cable, for example, is an Audio cable:

Listening to your output, you may have noticed something – you have entered short notes into the sequencer, but all the notes are playing until the next note comes in, and if you press Stop, the note continues to play.

From the knowledge you've gleaned reading this book so far, can you guess why that is and the next device that needs to be added? If you said an envelope, you'd be right! Without the envelope, the notes simply don't know when to stop.

Press another +, and add in a Decay Envelope, just to keep things simple:

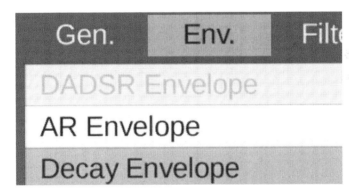

If you press Play, you will notice it's still done nothing!

This is because you need to connect it. Press Flip again, and then connect the Out from your Decay unit to the Mod of your oscillator.

What you're doing here is using the Output of the envelope to modify the envelope that the oscillator uses.

Next, filter your signal. Click on another +, and add a Vintage Ladder LP – a low-pass filter:

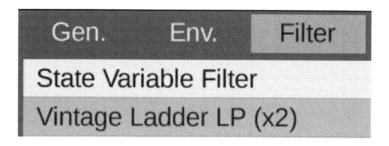

Switch your Waveform to sawtooth so you can hear the filter working (remember, it's defaulted to a sine wave, which lacks higher frequency harmonics):

And press Flip again!

Try to work out how you'd add a filter into the signal flow. I'll give you a clue – it's an Audio signal.

Check if you guessed correctly using this diagram:

To take stock, you now have an oscillator, which is being controlled by a Decay envelope, with its audio signal being filtered before it reaches the output.

Next, add an LFO. Click on the + again and select LFO:

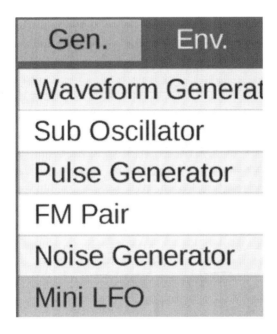

The LFO can be routed to the filter, as you already know – do this now:

Press Play, and then Flip. Alter your settings to make sure you can effectively hear the LFO acting upon the filter.

The beauty of this is that you can use routing creativity to modify other parameters. For example, Flip the setup back to the cabling view, and drag another cable from your LFO output to res on your filter:

If you press Flip again and turn the Res of your filter right up, you'll hear that now the LFO is not just acting upon your cutoff, but also your resonance – so the higher the value of your cutoff, the higher the value of your resonance.

The reason we have scratched the surface of virtual modular synthesis is to show you that synthesizer design is based on a simple set of connections. You should not be intimidated when you encounter this Doepfer A-100, as it is based on precisely the same principles that you've just learned:

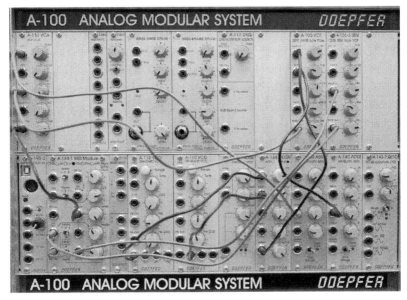

©Nina Richards / Wikimedia Commons / CC-BY-SA-3.0

Exercises – Q&A

1) Why do you need to add an envelope to prevent the notes blending into one another?

2) What are the two types of signal carried in the wires in Modular, and what are they for?

3) What sort of connection (i.e. Audio or Data) might there be between an Envelope and a Filter?

4) What sort of connection might there be between an LFO and an oscillator?

5) What sort of connection might there be between a Filter and the synthesizer's primary Output?

If you need any help, the answers are in Appendix A.

Exercises – Practice

1) Add an additional unit to your Caustic modular synthesizer, and connect it to your setup so that it works. Please note that if you add an additional sound-making module, you'll need to add a mixer to mix the two together!
2) Go to YouTube and watch a free modular synthesis tutorial.

Chapter 25– Other synthesizers

Throughout this book, I've used Caustic's SubSynth as the primary example of a synthesizer. However, all synthesizers have the same fundamental controls. This chapter is a series of exercises - I'd like you to have a look at the following synthesizers, deciphering where the where the various sections are. Try to identify the:

· Oscillators
· Oscillator mixer
· Filter
· Volume Envelope
· Filter Envelope

Here's a picture of ASynth, made by Smartelectronix:

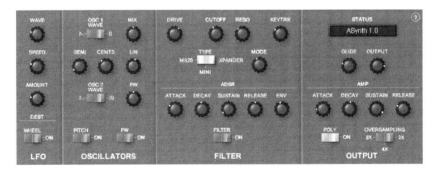

This one should be fairly easy – they've marked the areas out for you, however a couple of areas are slightly deceptive! Just in case you're not sure, here are the answers:

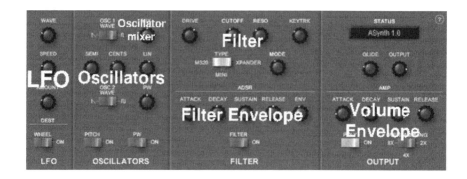

How about this one?

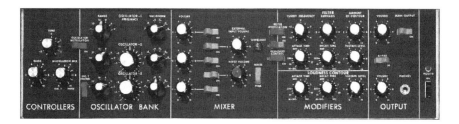

©Alex Harden / Wikimedia Commons / CC-BY-SA-3.0

It's easy when they're labeled, isn't it?

Let's try a more challenging one. I'll give you a clue – the full set of features you'd expect are not on this synthesizer:

©Steve Sims / Wikimedia Commons / CC-BY-SA-1.0

I told you this one was more challenging!

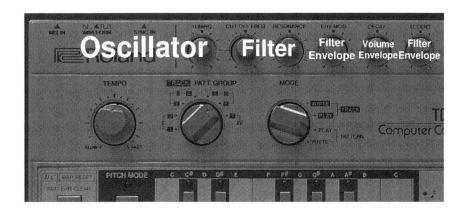

Let's try one more:

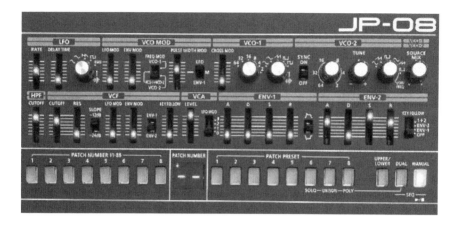

©Samboy / Wikimedia Commons / CC-BY-SA-1.0

Hopefully you found this one fairly easy – the only tricky part is realising that the envelopes are assignable, so envelope 1 can be assigned to control both the filter and the oscillator, and envelope can either control the filter or nothing:

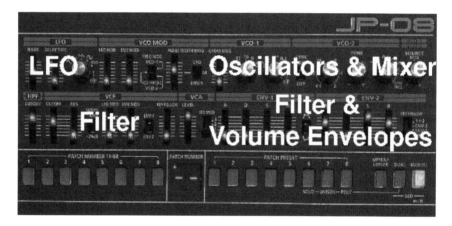

I hope you realise how simple it has been to decipher the different layouts of synthesizers – merely looking at them with an experienced, knowledgeable eye will give you an indication of how

212

they work. It's reassuring to know that all synthesis works using broadly the same architecture.

Exercises - Practice

1) Some synthesizers are detailed enough that they don't lend themselves to a book format well. For these exercises, I'd like you to find images of these synthesizers on the internet and use your newly found skills to decipher the constituent components of the following:

· Korg MS-20
· Native Instruments Massive
· Xfer Records Serum
· Doepfer A-100 (this is a particularly tough one – remember that there are several oscillators that perform different functions!)

Chapter 26 – Character

In this chapter, we're going to look at the character of different synthesizers and the effect that this character has on your productions.

In the sound creation chapters, you may have come very close to recreating some sounds you heard, but not quite managed to make them sound identical. This is because like any other musical instruments, different synthesizers sound different to one another – even if their control methods are similar.

Character is what differentiates different models of synthesizer. It is one of the most important aspects of electronic music production. The character of a synthesizer is a product of its design, its components and its software (if it has or is made from software). One of the primary attributes of character is whether a synthesizer is analogue or digital. Analogue means that its components are made out of real electronic chips, whereas digital can either mean that the synthesizer works on a computer platform, or that there are digital computing chips within the hardware synthesizer. There are a lot of modern, budget synthesizers which are a hybrid of the two – most often with a digital oscillator and an analogue filter (because it's the filter that can often add the most perceived character to a sound).

It is said (and I often agree) that analogue sounds better than digital synthesis. Analogue hardware is often described as sounding 'warm'. Scientifically, warmth is often a product of the analogue components of a piece of musical equipment creating a small amount of distortion, which adds pleasant-sounding harmonics. However, that's not to say that I haven't encountered cold-sounding analogue synthesizers and warm-sounding virtual synthesizers. To some extent, it's all a matter of preference.

Caustic's SubSynth is a very basic synthesizer, and has a very generic character. It's excellent for the experiments that we have undertaken in this book due to its sheer precision, but a wider variety of instruments would be necessary in a real music production environment.

Some of the most famous sounds in synthesis come from the character of a particular instrument. For example, the famous funky synthesizer lead sounds heard in *Parliament Funkadelic*'s work (and later used by G-Funk producers, especially Dre) are a product of the Minimoog synthesizer. Some of the most famous tracks of the 80s were produced using the FM-based Yamaha DX7 and its distinctive patches. Acid House - a whole genre of music - was invented as a consequence of the Roland 303 and its squelchy filters.

Character matters a lot in synthesis. Whilst I've written about the theory, the real learning is in undertaking the exercises in this chapter.

Exercises – Q&A

1) What are the three main aspects of a synthesizer's character?

215

2) What does analogue mean, when referring to a synthesizer?

3) What is 'warmth'?

If you need any help, the answers are in Appendix A.

Exercises – Practice

1) Use the internet to find videos the following synthesizers – I suggest you search for the synthesizer name, followed by 'Demo'. Use your active listening skills to listen for the distinctive character of these synthesizers:

· Minimoog

· Roland 303

· Access Virus TI

· Native Instruments Massive

While you're watching the videos, try to keep an eye out for the different sections of the synthesizer that we have worked on in previous chapters – this type of homework will stand you in good stead for the next chapter!

2) Listen to these tracks to hear the synthesizers in context (not all may be to your taste!):

· Minimoog – *Flashlight* by Parliament

· Roland 303 – *Acid Tracks* by Phuture

· Access Virus TI – *Invaders Must Die* by The Prodigy

· Native Instruments Massive – *The Reward Is Cheese* by Deadmau5

Chapter 27 - Experimenting with other synthesizers

In this chapter, we're going to use another of Caustic's synthesizers to apply our knowledge. Think of this as a final examination, just to test how far you've come on this journey.

Go to Caustic, and then load up a SawSynth (instead of a SubSynth). Using the experience and knowledge you've gained, decipher each section of the synthesizer and its function. As you'll appreciate from the chapter on other synthesizers, you may note that there is a different layout and a different-looking oscillator. Don't worry - this is part of your journey.

The reason I spent so much time teaching you about SubSynth is so that when you're presented with a new synthesizer, it's not intimidating. I know this is counterintuitive, but by fully understanding precisely what an oscillator does, you've learned how *all* oscillators work. By putting in the practice to understand exactly how SubSynth's envelope works, you've learned how *all* envelopes work.

What's new is the Super Osc:

Experiment with it, try to work out scientifically what it's doing differently to SubSynth's oscillator.

If you're not sure, here's a spoiler - it creates multiples of the waveform selected. Then, it detunes them according to the extent of the Detune slider. The higher the Mix, the more multiples of oscillators are played. The higher the Detune slider, the more these are detuned against each other, creating that lovely harmonic interference. If you're not sure what Detune is - it's just the oscillator being played at a slightly different frequency, just like moving the Cents pot slightly on SubSynth.

If you're looking to find out more about the concept behind Caustic's Super Osc, search for information on Roland's *SuperSaw* oscillator on the internet.

You should also note the filter envelope. Whereas SubSynth employed an inverted filter to work with the envelope, the filter envelope on SawSynth has no effect at midday:

218

Applies an upward filter movement if it is set to the right of midday:

And applies a downward filter movement (just like the inverted filter in SubSynth) if set to the left of midday:

Again, these are minor changes to your workflow, yet fundamentally it's performing precisely the same function - it's simply the method that has changed slightly.

Now you're familiar with SawSynth, I'm going to set you the challenge of creating two patches from scratch. I'll give you the notes to program into the sequencer, and a vague reference to the sound I'm looking for but then it's all up to you. We'll compare patches after you've created yours.

Firstly, I want you to create a floaty, ethereal pad. Here are your notes:

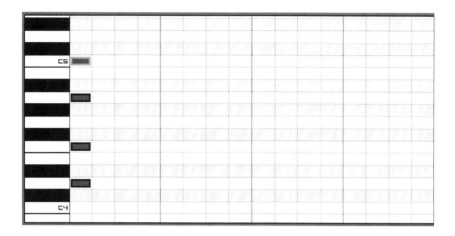

In order to create the right note length for your pad, simply to go the top of the sequencer and click on the Size button:

Then, drag the right side of the notes to the right, one at a time, until you have a full bar of notes:

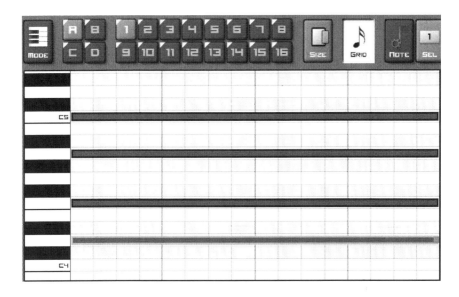

Now play your pad, and while it loops, experiment until you find a result you believe sounds right.

Here's what I came up with:

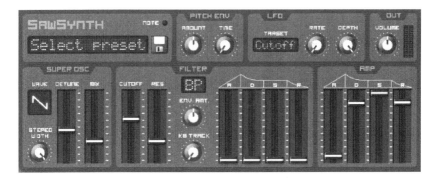

Of course, we're firmly within the realms of subjectivity here, so if you believe yours sounds good, then well done! However, make a note of the key features I've employed just to make sure your rationale was correct:

· Sawtooth wave - this is due to the harmonics it creates.

· High stereo width - this contributes to the ethereal feeling. Stereo width works by separating the copies of detuned soundwaves between your left and right speakers, making the overall sound more expansive.

· Detune just below halfway, with Mix a quarter of the way up - enough to add some harmonic interference, but not so much that it sounds hugely detuned.

· Band-pass filter with a slow LFO - so that the pad moves and undulates in the upper-mid range.

· No filter envelope applied - this is to allow the LFO to perform the undulation without competing with the filter envelope.

· Fast attack, but long Sustain and Release to allow each cycle of the bar being played to work as seamlessly as possible.

Next, I want you to create an EDM lead. Create a new instance of SubSynth, and load these notes:

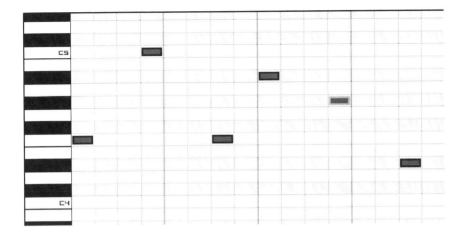

For an example of a classic EDM lead, listen to the lead in *Levels* by *Avicii*.

As you know from the chapter on leads, leads are fairly easy to program - the trick in getting this right is to add the correct amount of detune so that the lead sounds wild, but not too wild. Here's what I came up with:

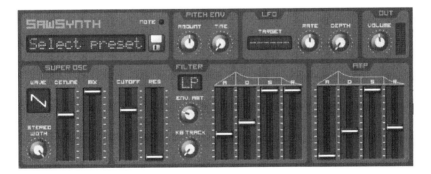

To note:

· I've used a sawtooth again, maximising the stereo width.

223

· Detune is just beyond halfway, adding a lot of detune but without going too far. The detune is mixed in with the original signal to the maximum possible extent.

· I've added a low-pass filter with a fairly slow filter envelope, so that it acts upon the sound slowly. This isn't essential, but I find it gives the lead a little bit of movement.

· The lead has quick Attack, with Sustain at full volume. This combines with a fairly slow Release, enabling the note to hang in the air slightly as it elapses.

You're entirely welcome to season these sounds using effects as you see fit, but now you've acquired real-world practice in applying your knowledge of synthesis to a new, unfamiliar synthesizer.

If your patches didn't precisely mirror mine, that's ok - as long as you were able to confidently use the different functions of the synthesizer, carrying into the chapter a good mental model of what each function does.

If you feel like you failed this chapter miserably, that's also ok - but I suggest you head back to Chapter 3 and re-work your way through the book, paying particular attention to the exercises.

It's now up to you to complete the exercises at the end of this chapter. You should be aware that these exercises are a lot tougher and will take you longer than the previous exercises in this book - think of it as your final project!

Exercises – Q&A

1) What does Super Osc do?

2) What's the difference between the filter envelope in SawSynth and the filter envelope in SubSynth?

3) What does Stereo Width do?

4) Why would you want to add some Release to the EDM lead?

If you need any help, the answers are in Appendix A.

Exercises – Practice

1) Find three synthesizers you would like to use. They could be online, at a local music shop, or as part of a software package.

2) Create three patches on each of these - a bass, a lead and a pad. Only skip a task if the synthesizer is wholly unsuited to the job (e.g. a pad on a monophonic bass synthesizer). Even if you struggle with the first synthesizer, I have no doubt that you will feel confident by the third.

Chapter 28 - Concluding thoughts

Thank you for reading this book and undertaking this journey.

To be clear, I don't doubt that if you were new to synthesis at the start of the book, you're still not one hundred percent confident by now. That's ok - no book can turn you into an expert overnight. It's important to remember that you will never stop learning about synthesis for as long as you practice it. The best way to practice it is to free yourself from the self-imposed shackles of relying on online tutorials and trying to edit presets. There's a wealth of undiscovered sound out there, and the knowledge in this book is more than enough for you to go out and discover it!

I do hope that the theory and exercises in this book have made you realise the beautiful simplicity of synthesis. A synthesizer is just like any other device, for example a car, a smartphone, a cooker, in that once you've learned the basics of one, you can apply that knowledge to any other.

I also hope that the journey you've undertaken has been worthwhile for you. For me, the journey of learning synthesis has been one of liberation. Because I feel confident programming and understanding synthesizers, I know that *any* synthesized sound I hear, be it in a track I hear in a record shop, a lead synth I hear at a gig or even the background music on television, is merely a combination of a particular programmed patch and the synthesizer's internal character.

Therefore, there is no sound that is truly out of my reach as a producer.

As an electronic musician, is there anything more liberating than that?

Appendix A – Q&A Exercise answers

1) Sound is a pressure wave that ripples out from a source.

2) Frequency, amplitude and waveform.

3) Hertz.

4) Hertz measures how many cycles are in the waveform per second.

5) 20Hz-20kHz.

Chapter 3 – What Is Synthesis?

1) An oscillator generates an electronic vibration at a set frequency according to a set waveform.

2) An amplifier increases the volume of the oscillator and outputs the amplified signal. The signal becomes audible through the speakers connected to the synthesizer, which convert the electronic signals to audible sound.

3) The creation of sound, followed by the manipulation of the sound created.

Chapter 5 – An Introduction to Caustic

1) LFO 2

2) Filter

Chapter 6 - Single Oscillators

1) Sine, Sawtooth, Square, Triangle, Noise

2) Saw

3) Square

4) Noise

5) Sine

6) Sawtooth

Chapter 7 – Mixing oscillators

1) It moves the oscillator in question up or down a semitone, as if you're playing the note above or below the note you're actually playing on the keyboard.

2) It moves the oscillator in question up or down an octave, as if you're playing the same note, but one octave above or below the note you're actually playing on the keyboard.

3) It moves the oscillator in question up or down a fraction of a semitone.

4) Bend makes the notes 'bend' between notes.

5) You would use the Phase pot to change where the peaks and troughs land in relation to each other.

Chapter 8 – Filters

1) Low-pass, band-pass and high-pass
2) High frequencies
3) It amplifies (i.e. increases in volume) frequencies around the filter's cut-off point
4) Track increases or decreases the amount of filter applied to the sound, depending on the note played

Chapter 9 – Envelopes

1) Release
2) Attack
3) Sustain
4) Decay

Chapter 10 – Filter Envelopes

1) Attack
2) Change the filter type to Inv. LP
3) Bring the filter envelope controls to the left of 12 o'clock, as 12 o'clock would have no effect

Chapter 11 – LFOs

1) Low Frequency Oscillator

2) A normal oscillator creates an audio signal, whereas an LFO creates an internal signal to manipulate certain controls within the synthesizer.

3) The Rate pot changes the speed of the LFO, i.e. the speed of the effect.

4) The Depth pot changes the extent to which the LFO effects its destination.

Chapter 12 – Polyphony

1) Monophonic means the synthesizer can only play one note at a time

2) Polyphonic means the synthesizer can play multiple notes at the same time

3) Turn the polyphony down to 1

Chapter 13 – Effects

1) Delay and modulation

2) Compression effects

3) Modulation effects

4) Equalization

Chapter 14 – Delay Effects

1) Because the Delay is repeating copies of the sound over the current sound.

2) It governs how long a sound will be captured and repeated.

3) Feedback governs how quickly (or slowly) the volume of subsequent repetitions are reduced.

4) Because the repetitions are reducing in volume so slowly, each new repetition builds on top of the last one - creating an increase in volume

5) Because Wet/Dry is the mix between your original signal and your effected sound. Moving it all the way to Wet means you only hear the output of your effect, effectively mixing out your original sound.

6) So that you can hear the effect of the Reverb in isolation, without the Delay getting in the way of you hearing what's reverb and what isn't.

7) Because Reverb is designed to simulate your sound being played in a reverberant room

8) Delay controls how long a delay the echoes are delayed for before they are mixed in with the output.

9) By creating a difference between the left and right speaker, it sounds like the sound occupies a wider, more realistic space.

10) Because the signal will be effected as it goes through the chain of effects units. For example, if you'd u had a Reverb and then a Delay, the signal would include Reverb as it enters the Delay, meaning the Reverb echoes would also be subject to the Delay's effects.

Chapter 15 – Modulation effects

1) Depth controls the extent the LFO is applied to the chorus, whereas Wet/Dry controls the extent that the effected signal is mixed with the unaffected signal.

2) A Delay unit delays the sound at fixed intervals, making each delay quieter than the last, however the Chorus delays the sound at 30-50 millisecond, with no repetitions.

3) Because the sound waves constructively and destructively interfere with one another.

4) Because two identical sounds more than 50ms apart will be perceived by the brain as two separate sounds.

5) F.Back controls the extent to which the effected signal is pumped back into itself.

6) A flanger varies the time between two signals, whereas a phaser changes the phase.

7) Because they all create their effects by creating identical copies of your sound, delayed by time - the difference is the extent of the timing.

Chapter 16 – Equalization

1) Parametric equalization allows you to pick the frequency range you alter

2) The display shows the user visually how the parametric equalizer is affecting the signal

3) The Frequency pot allows the user to choose which frequency is to be affected.

4) This allows the user to choose how much of the frequency range is boosted or cut around the centre point chosen by Frequency.

5) This allows the user to increase or decrease the amount of the frequency selected by the Frequency pot, by the amount selected by the Gain pot.

6) Because the lower end of the sequence/melody may interfere with the bassline

Chapter 17 – Compression

1) Compression quietens the loud sound, so that it's at a similar level to the quiet sound.

2) Dynamic range is the difference in volume between the loudest and quietest part of a track.

3) Threshold controls the level at which the signal passes through unaffected – any signal louder than the threshold level gets compressed.

4) Because the setting of the threshold is so high, none of the signal meets it.

5) Ratio is the extent to which the compressor reduces the volume of anything above the level set by the Threshold.

6) 1/3 of the original volume.

7) Attack controls how long it takes the compressor to start compressing once a signal above the Threshold has been detected.

8) Release controls how long it takes the compressor to cease compressing once a signal above the Threshold has been detected.

9) Sidechain is where a compressor is triggered by an external signal, as opposed to the audio signal routed into the compressor.

10) Basses, pads and noise sweeps.

11) A Limiter has a fixed ratio, and is designed to prevent any signal from breaching the threshold.

12) Pre-defines the extent to which audio is amplified before it enters the Limiter. Post defines the extent to which the audio is amplified after it has been processed by the Limiter.

Chapter 18 – Creating a bass

1) To temper the high end of the bass, so that it isn't *too* bright.

a) Selecting oscillators with harmonics, i.e. sawtooth and square waves

b) Adding some Attack to the inv. LP filter

c) Moving Cents on Oscillator 2 to create interference

d) Adjusting the volume envelope

e) Adding an LFO to the Filter cutoff

3) Because basses are intended to be heard at the lower end, thereby underpinning the track.

4) A sub-bass underpins the whole track, but is at a lower frequency than a bass and doesn't draw too much attention to itself. It's designed to be felt more than heard.

Chapter 19 – Creating a Pad

1) Pads are created to be slow-moving and lush – and therefore require long note lengths.

2) Why would you want to use a Band Pass filter for a pad?

2) Pads often work in the middle-high area of the audible frequency range, which is what a Band Pass filter allows through.

3) So that the filter rises with every new note.

4) Why did I choose to alter the phase of oscillator 2 using an LFO instead of changing it on LFO2's settings?

5) Being Delay effects, the evolution of the sound can be captured and reflected back and forth, creating more harmonic lushness.

Chapter 20 – Creating a Lead

1) So that you're always playing one note at a time – even if you accidentally play two notes!

2) It means that if you're using a touchscreen or mouse, you can naturally navigate notes that sound good together.

3) Polyphony set to 1, a sawtooth, and hitting the right notes (thanks to the change in scale).

4) Sawtooth

5) Sine

Chapter 21 – Creating chords

1) Chords are a group of notes (typically three or more) played at once to create a harmony.

2) So that the movement of the cutoff creates drama – and it does so in addition to your movement of the cutoff.

3) This creates additional depth by essentially doubling your chord – playing a copy of it an octave lower means that six notes are being played, instead of three.

4) This is so that you can fully hear each effect of each pot turn – you can then combine it with the unaltered signal by moving it back when you've found the right sound.

Chapter 22 – Recreating sounds

1) Because the Release closes down the volume envelope so instantaneously that it creates an audible click due to the speed at which the waveform ceases to play.

2) Sustain would make the Decay sound like it's been lengthened slightly and a high Release setting would mean you could hear the note after it's been played.

3) Because a slow attack means the notes fade in – the fact that the notes in Three Drives' riff don't therefore indicates a fast Attack.

4) The sound seems to be bright at the start of a note but loses its brightness as the note goes on – in a similar way to a piano note.

5) The sub-bass is set at such a low frequency that the frequencies are too low for a low-pass filter to have any effect – therefore Volume is the parameter that needs modulating.

6) It contains a lot of bass weight, but also some harmonics, which sound great when filtered and modulated.

Chapter 23 – Drum synthesis

1) The Tune pot defines the frequency at which the sample plays.

237

2) The Punch pot acts as an Attack envelope, defining how quickly the sample gets to peak volume.

3) The Decay pot acts as a Decay envelope, defining how quickly the sample returns to zero volume

4) The Pan pot controls the mix of the sample between the left and right speaker.

5) The volume pot controls the volume of the sample.

6) Noise shaping is turning white noise into a sound with character, for example a percussive sound.

7) Because the envelopes allow you to add shape to the noise as it's played, as opposed to it being a flat blast of white noise.

Chapter 24 – Routing Matrices

1) Because without the envelope, there's nothing to tell the notes when to stop.

2) Audio and Data. Audio carries pure audio signals, whereas Data (also known as CV) carries signals to alter particular parameters.

3) Data, because the data from the Envelope would control how the Filter is applied.

4) Data, because the data from the LFO would control how the LFO alters the oscillator.

5) Audio, because it would route the audio directly from the output of the filter to the synthesizer's output.

Chapter 26 – Character

1) Its components, its design and its software (if it has software).
238

2) Analogue means the synthesizer's components are made out of real electronic chips.

3) Warmth is analogue components adding a small amount of distortion to the signal, creating pleasant harmonics.

Chapter 27 – Experimenting with other synthesizers

1) Super Osc creates multiples of the waveform selected, detuning each copy slightly to create pleasant harmonic interference.

2) Whereas the filter envelope on SubSynth uses inverted filters to create opposite effects, the opposite filter envelope effect on SawSynth can be achieved by moving the filter envelope to the left or right of midnight.

3) Stereo Width separates the copies of detuned sawtooth waves between the left and right speakers, creating a more spacious, expansive sound.

4) This allows the note to slightly hang in the air after it elapses.

Appendix B – Areas and functions of Caustic

The part with SubSynth and Init written below SubSynth is the patch section. This is unmarked. This is where you will load and save different settings into your synthesizer –q not unlike the File menu on most computer programs.

Oscillator 1 and Oscillator 2 – these are below the patch section. These are the Oscillators – the part of the synthesizer that generates sound – the sound that you will manipulate and shape into the sound you desire.

Bend – this is where you control how different notes interact tonally with one another.

Filter (to the right of the patch section) – this is a section that lets you selectively control which frequencies from the oscillator get played. This is where you give your sound tone, character and warmth. You can also manipulate how and when the filter is applied using the Envelope controls (the four pots in the section titled Attack, Decay, Sustain and Release).

LFO 1 and LFO 2, to the right of the filter. This is where you can choose various waveforms and drive them towards other parts of the synthesizer to create automated effects. Don't worry if this explanation doesn't make sense at this point – all will become clear once you've worked through the LFO chapter!

The Volume Envelope. This is where you control note-level parameters, such as whether your notes are short or long, whether they start slowly or quickly after you press a key on the keyboard and whether they continue playing after you've ceased to press a note on the keyboard. This allows you to create slow, relaxed notes, or aggressive, fast notes – or anything in between!

The Output. This is simply how loud your synthesizer is. Nice and easy!

The keyboard section. This piano keyboard is where you tell the synthesizer which notes to play. If you're on a touch device, you can touch the keys with your finger on the screen, or if you're on a desktop computer you can use the mouse, your computer keyboard or a connected MIDI keyboard.

Index

242

Dubstep, 72
dynamic range, 120, 121, 122, 141

EQ, 33, 35, 36, 38, 39, 52, 54, 55, 84, 85, 114, 115, 116, 117, 118, 119, 147, 152, 154, 170
Equalisation, 85, 246
Equalization, 111

Faithless, 184, 186, 187
fifth chord, 75, 85
filter envelope, 56, 68, 69, 70, 71, 76, 80, 85, 145, 160, 176, 190, 231, 234, 236, 237, 243, 253
Frequency, 10
Frequency Modulation, 47
frequency spectrum, 116
Funkadelic, 82, 165, 226

Gain, 112, 113, 114, 116, 118, 247
gain reduction, 127, 128, 129, 130, 138, 139, 140, 142
Garage, 72

hardware, 4, 13, 19, 48, 80, 92, 209, 225, 226
harmonic, 36, 40, 54, 144, 145, 150, 151, 156, 159, 161, 162, 172, 193, 230, 234, 249, 253
harmonic content, 40, 144, 145, 150, 151, 156, 193
harmonically rich, 38, 158, 175, 189
harmonics, 36, 37, 38, 39, 40, 44, 47, 54, 152, 186, 192, 194, 216, 226, 234, 248, 251, 253
Harmonics, 36
Hertz, 10, 11, 14, 241
high-pass filter, 50
hip hop, 82
House, 72, 82, 174, 226

Init, 27, 29, 30, 51, 74, 85, 143, 149, 157, 165, 184, 188, 194
Initial patch, 29
interference, 45, 99, 101, 102, 103, 107, 146, 159, 161, 162, 172, 178, 230, 234, 249, 253

Joris Voorn, 137

Kahn, 150
Kraftwerk, 165, 204

loudness war, 122

243

KDRT

Printed in Poland
by Amazon Fulfillment
Poland Sp. z o.o., Wrocław

52771743R00141